Christopher Lehman

ENERGIZE
RESEARCH READING & WRITING

Fresh Strategies to Spark Interest, Develop Independence, and Meet Key Common Core Standards

GRADES **4–8**

Foreword by Lucy Calkins

HEINEMANN
Portsmouth, NH

Heinemann
361 Hanover Street
Portsmouth, NH 03801–3912
www.heinemann.com

Offices and agents throughout the world

The author and publisher wish to thank those who have generously given permission to reprint borrowed material:

Excerpts from *Common Core State Standards* © Copyright 2010. National Governors Association Center for Best Practices and Council of Chief State School Officers. All rights reserved.

Library of Congress Cataloging-in-Publication Data
Lehman, Christopher.
   Energize research reading and writing : fresh strategies to spark interest, develop independence, and meet key common core standards, grades 4–8 / Christopher Lehman ; foreword by Lucy Calkins.
       p. cm.
   Includes bibliographical references.
   ISBN-13: 978-0-325-04357-9
   ISBN-10: 0-325-04357-4
   1. Language arts (Elementary). 2. Language arts (Middle school).   I. Title.
LB1576.L3756 2012
372.6—dc23   2012011860

Editor: Tobey Antao
Production: Victoria Merecki
Cover and interior designs: Monica Ann Crigler
Typesetter: Cape Cod Compositors, Inc.
Front cover photo: © 2006 Rubberball/HIP
Back cover photo: Yesenia Garcia
Manufacturing: Steve Bernier

Printed in the United States of America on acid-free paper

21 20 19 18 17   VP   5 6 7 8 9

To Yesenia.
For It All.

CONTENTS

Chapter 4   61

Beyond "Put It into Your Own Words": *Teach Students to Write to Teach Ideas, Not Just Regurgitate Facts*

Chapter 5   87

Free from Graphic Organizers: *Teach Students to Craft Organizing Structures with Their Readers in Mind*

Chapter 6   113

Without Agonizing Memorization: *Teach Students to Cite Sources on Their Own*

FOREWORD

Look over your shelves of professional books. There are the beautifully written pages by writers like Georgia Heard and Katherine Bomer. These are the books we turn to when we need reminders of why we chose this profession, when we find ourselves needing to remember that the work we do is not just a job, it's a calling. These books help us to feel, inside our chest, a great, welling sense of life purpose.

Then there are those call-it-like-it-is books that startle us with the way they capture the absolute honest truth of teaching. They don't dress teaching up. They don't pretend that all our lesson plans work or that all our kids will listen intently and then eagerly traipse off to work on everything we ask them to do. Instead, they are filled with students who are as real and as funny and as challenging as the impossible, difficult, wonderful children who keep us sleepless at night. These books make us feel less crazy and less alone. They make us laugh at the absurdity of the jobs we are asked to do, even as we work intensely to do them better.

Of course, you also have how-to books on your shelves. They may even be the most dog-eared, as these days we are asked to somehow be miracle workers in every area of curriculum possible. The only way to pull it off, frankly, is to lean on books full of classroom-tested, ever-so-practical strategies. These books usually cut to the chase. They have charts full of great ideas and lists of tips, resources, and techniques. We duplicate pages of these books to distribute at grade-level meetings. It's illegal, we realize, as we stand in front of the duplicating machine, but so what? Arrest me for wanting to teach well and for wanting my colleagues to do so as well.

Then there are the books that give us philosophies that anchor us. They tend to be slim, which is a good thing because we can only read them in small doses. One can only take in so much at a time of Jerome Bruner's *Process of Education*. But these are the books we call on when we need to chart our course in the world. They give us words that clarify our stances and inform our choices.

Here's the reason I love Chris Lehman's newest book: it is all those books rolled into one. There are patches of sheer beauty, places where you find yourself believing that teaching kids to conduct research is not just a requirement of the Common Core but is, instead, one of the most important gifts we can possibly give to our children. Then there are the down-and-dirty sections in which Chris could absolutely be the teacher next door, the one who is always cracking you up with his witty comments about kids and teaching and the pressures of today.

Those parts provide the framework. The real stuff comes in the pages that brim with ideas for how to transform research from those reports of yesteryear to something current and vital and important and, yes, aligned with the Common Core. Then, too, there are the small sections in which this book speaks beyond research and comments on all of teaching, addressing the values and choices that undergird everything we do.

You'll probably read this book because it is absolutely the right book at the right time. The Common Core State Standards require that you and your colleagues think carefully about ways you can make research—especially the quick, everyday sorts of research that are the trademark of any scholarly life—into your classroom. But you'll reread this book, share it—and, yes, duplicate its pages—because Chris is able to be a pastor, a keynote speaker, a witty and blunt confidante, a generous coach and mentor, a philosopher . . . and he makes us know that we can be all these things as well. After all, the trademark of great teaching is that we can assume these different roles when our students need us to do so.

—**Lucy Calkins**

ACKNOWLEDGMENTS

Whenever I hear someone refer to teachers as being "on the frontlines" I cringe a little. Who are they fighting, anyway? The students?

This day, though, that metaphor is ringing more true. Within a world that seems to be continually in flux and a climate that is whipping education into a frenzy, we *are* on the frontlines. We fight alongside our students, their families, our colleagues, and anyone who would care to join. In this profession we fight until every child, everywhere in the world, is educated, well fed, and strong. No one disagrees that learning can, should, go even better. But I raise this question: when have teachers ever stopped aiming to improve?

I would first like to extend my gratitude to just some of the many educators I have been lucky enough to work alongside. You have shaped me, just as you shape your students and this profession.

First, thanks to the many literacy coaches and coordinators that make the world go round: Brian Sweeney, Brenda Dolan, Maureen Cassarino, Kendall Latham, Belinda Bean (and Brazilian lunch), Maysoon Massoud, Taraf Ghanem, Cynthia Augello, Nora Lichtenstein, Jane Wind, Carrie Tenebrini, Sheila Mason, Michael Flaherty, Barb Rogers, Kathleen Mallon, Elizabeth Lacey—when do any of you ever sleep? Barbara Newkirk for reviewing versions of chapters and for ever-positive support. Ronda Baker for your passionate and steadfast belief in all learners—child and adult alike. Each one of you is a rock your colleagues stand upon; you raise us all higher.

Hundreds of teachers impact my thinking, daily. Amidst data and phone calls, meetings and memos, you still save the greatest dose of energy for your students. I have witnessed miracle moments in the lives of young people at your hands. Particular thanks to Barbara Makrogiannis, Kevin Hernandez, Ryan Dunbar, Ben Raikes, Dana Stachowiak, Rebecca Victoros, and Gabby Deveaux, for your efforts for this book and in your classrooms. As well as teams that help me study and reflect including those at IS 230, MS 67, St. Hope Leadership Academy, Union County Public Schools, Orchard Valley Middle School, Our World Neighborhood Middle School, Burnet Hill Elementary School, Woodward Parkway Elementary School, PS/MS 19, Muskego-Norway Schools, Taipei American School, the Queen Rania Teacher Academy, and hosts of others.

And, essentially, the vision-focused administrators that dare to publically learn, lead, and take risks. You are under the pressure of the world and yet manage to hold back the dark clouds so students and teachers can shine. In particular my gratitude goes to Sharon Terry, Ron Zirin, Lisa Steiger, Elaine Bakke, Patrick Klocek, Trish O'Regan, Montrio Belton, Kevin Plue, and John Jones for years of partnership, example, and more importantly, your continued bravery.

Equally on these frontlines are the literacy leaders I have come to call family. Thanks to Lucy Calkins, for your leadership, your insight, and endless drive. I have come to find the engine of your work is your undying mission that every child has a voice. I am tremendously thankful for your mentoring and belief. Thanks as well to the tirelessly working leaders at the Reading and Writing Project and to my fellow Staff Developers: I know no more caring and passionate people all collected in one place than here.

I would not be able to publically join in this education conversation if not for my friends at Heinemann. Enormous thanks to Kate Montgomery for first seeing the potential in these ideas and most importantly, for connecting me with the greatest editor known to man, Tobey Antao.

Tobey, I think I need seven more pages to appropriately thank you for your wisdom, kindness, and wit. I left every conversation feeling more energized than before. You always kindly suggested any revisions were my own—but I'm on to you, it was your talents that make the final version of this book as much yours as mine. It is such a gift to work with you.

Victoria Merecki, production editor extraordinaire, I do not know how you have your pulse on every point—every word—so well, and to you and Monica Crigler for the exciting design. David Cottingham, I can't think of any less interesting task than correcting my errors, yet you did more than just look for dangling modifiers—you brought your keen, artful eye for the experience readers will have with this text. And thanks to every working magician behind the scenes in production.

I close with the most important people, *mi corazón*: Yesenia, Tahlya, and Marcos. It feels fitting that you are in mind as the page turns and the book begins. When people have asked me, "How do you write *and* have a family?" it is truthfully a hard question to answer. Hours in front of the computer are hours not together. I am grateful for the times you let me lock myself in a room—and more so those times when you did not. A walk together through the aquarium or spaghetti around the corner is my lifeblood. All I do is for you and from you.

ENERGIZE

RESEARCH READING & WRITING

CHAPTER 1

Research the Way It Was Meant to Be

A Re-Introduction

Researchers are game changers, innovators. Research—be it that of scientists, historians, journalists, musicians, architects, artists, doctors, or teachers—is the way we as humans evolve. Literally. Our life expectancy is longer than ever, recent technological achievements compete with science fiction, and the amount we collectively know and share is greater than at any time in history.

Now, with this in mind, with all the exciting, glorious, thank-you-for-your-gifts-to-the-world feelings welling up inside of you, pause. Shift your thoughts to school, to rows of students doing "research projects."

I'll give you a moment to recover.

Walk the hallways of almost any school and there is a good chance that colorful (and well-intended) projects will line the halls or hang from classroom walls and ceilings: mobiles of famous historical figures, essays on science phenomena, reports on authors in English Language Arts. But look closer, past the clip art and poster board, and you will probably find that most of these "projects" contain, at worst, text lifted directly from sources or, at best, lists of dry facts in the general shape of paragraphs—both of which, let's be honest, are an incredible bore to read. What's even worse, walk over to that project's creator and ask her to tell you what she learned, and in many instances she will talk broadly, cautiously about the generalities of her topic, but will lack the depth of knowledge the time spent working on that project should have delivered. Too often, what students produce at the end of a "research project" is little more than proof that they skimmed a few books or web pages and took some notes. Research becomes a task to complete, not a means of deep committed learning, not a drive to inform others.

This book is intended to be a call for research the way it was meant to feel, for reading and writing about research to matter to our students—to give them the tools needed to be successful learners and leaders in college and beyond. This is an argument for making our teaching of research warmly invite our children and young adults into the fold of inquisitive, innovative thinkers. It is intended to teach research skills in ways that encourage engagement and independence.

Standards and Testing Highlight the Essential Role of Research Skills

Echoing this call for meaningful research instruction is the Common Core State Standards and the new standardized tests, both of which see research skills as integral to college and career readiness. An entire strand of the writing standards K–12 is devoted to "Research to Build and Present Knowledge," and in general many other "skills important to research are infused throughout the document" (p. 8). The standards expect students to learn to *independently* use a whole host of research-related skills, to be able to do things such as:

- "conduct short as well as more sustained research projects" (writing standard 7)
- "gather relevant information from multiple print and digital sources" (writing standard 8)
- "integrate and evaluate content presented in diverse formats" (reading standards 7, 9, writing standard 8, speaking and listening standards 2, 3)
- "assess the credibility and accuracy of each source" (writing standard 8, reading standard 7)
- "acquire and use accurately a range of general academic and domain-specific words and phrases" (language standard 6)
- "draw evidence from literary or informational texts" (writing standard 9, *which references that students must use the skills of all 10 reading standards!*)

They must then be able to use all of the above to produce a range of writing and speaking types and genres (writing standards 1, 2, even 3; speaking and listening standards 4, 5,

6; language standards 1, 2, 3) through an internalized writing process (writing standards 4, 5, 6).

Phew.

It is not surprising, then, that the two groups developing the standardized tests that aim to assess student progress with the Common Core State Standards are also highlighting research skills. Nearly half of CCSS adopting states have joined the PARCC (Partnership for Assessment of Readiness for College and Careers), which states that a key piece of students' standardized tests will be "performance-based assessments" of which they plan one to be a "research simulation task" where "the student will demonstrate the ability to read and comprehend a range of sufficiently complex texts independently, to write effectively when using and analyzing sources, and to build and present knowledge through integration, comparison, and synthesis of ideas" (p. 2, PARCC Item Development ITN FAQs, Dec. 2011). Other CCSS adopting states are members of the SMARTER Balanced Assessment Consortium, with some states acting as members of both groups. In a recent draft of their "Content Specifications," this group explains that they intend to highlight research within the assessment, giving students an "Inquiry/Research Score" making up one of five areas that will add up to a student's total assessment score. As with PARCC, students taking this test will again most likely be involved with "extended response/performance tasks," where students might read or view informational articles or personal accounts "and then be asked to respond to a research question posed" or even "collaboratively generate and explore a variety of potential digital and print resources," and then "individually, students [will] prepare and present their results to show that they can draw conclusions that integrate or analyze information" (pp. 49–50, September 19, 2011 v19.0).

In essence, the standards and the tests that will assess them are expecting that students become researchers—not graphic organizer filler-in-ers, not text copiers, but independently thinking, curious, and rigorous researchers. Taking time to teach students to research well is taking time to teach them the skills of the standards. Teaching students to research well is teaching them to learn well.

Using This Book to Energize Your Teaching

Cover to cover, this book aims to tell a new story of more engaged, more student-driven, more independent research instruction. It is written to also serve as a friend on the shelf that you turn to with a specific need, jumping to a particular section to find the right strategy for the right lesson.

Chapters 2–6 are divided into some of our greatest concerns when it comes to the teaching of research skills: from helping students find their own sources to teaching students to cite accurately. Each chapter is full of fresh, practical strategies to support you in teaching research skills that help students become more independent researchers.

Chapter 7, "English or Content Areas, Long Studies or Short Projects: Turn Strategies into a Study That Matches the Needs in Your Classroom," then aims to help you put everything together, helping you to use the strategies described in the book to plan either full, multi-week studies or short research projects.

Differentiating Research Across Content Areas, Across Many Grades

A particular aim of this book is to support you in making choices. There is no one-size-fits-all magic cure for reaching all learners; instead, it takes smart teachers, like you, making decisions based on the needs of your students. As a Staff Developer with the Reading and Writing Project, I have been lucky enough to study with hundreds of teachers in elementary and middle schools, in English, Social Studies, and Science classrooms and to ponder, study, and revise issues facing students in the company of my colleagues. What I have learned from living within communities of educators is that good teaching is good teaching, no matter what the content. The methods of clear and engaging instruction apply across grade levels. The difference comes not in how you teach, but in what you say—both the language you use and the rigor of strategies.

To support you in making decisions for your classroom, there are a few features throughout the chapters:

- **Samples of grade-level language used in teaching examples:** Whenever I include sample language for lessons, I begin by telling you the grade level in which that language was used. When you see, "When teaching a class of fourth graders, I might say . . ." it doesn't mean seventh graders cannot use that strategy, it is just to indicate the age level of the descriptions and examples used in the demonstration. I always aim to speak to older students as young adults and to make sure that examples with younger students match what they could do themselves. Adjust any example to meet the needs of your class.

- **A range of content examples:** To show how these strategies might live in an English Language Arts, Social Studies, or Science study, throughout the book a variety of content examples are given, from researching historical events, to science concepts, to living things. They are intended to help you see your own course material throughout the book, but are provided only as examples.

- **At-a-glance guide for differentiation:** At the start of every main topic you will see a progression that suggests a simple three-level range of instruction, from "teaching for more emergent researchers" up to "teaching for more experienced researchers." It is there to show how ideas from the upcoming section could be targeted to the needs of your students. (See Figure 1–1.) If your students have more emergent research skills, then read the first box for a general image of the ways you might adjust your instruction to support their development. With that image in mind you will be better equipped to decide which strategies to select for your class and which to either skip over or change.

- **Additional strategies for your particular needs:** Each of the strategies described within a chapter is followed by a text box with information to support you in differentiating for your students. (See Figure 1–2.) The section provides

Differentiating Instruction

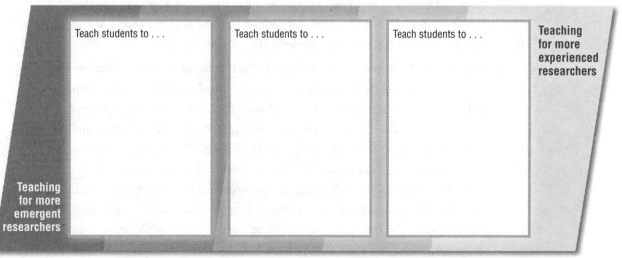

Teach students to . . .

Teach students to . . .

Teach students to . . .

Teaching for more experienced researchers

Teaching for more emergent researchers

Figure 1–1

Figure 1–2

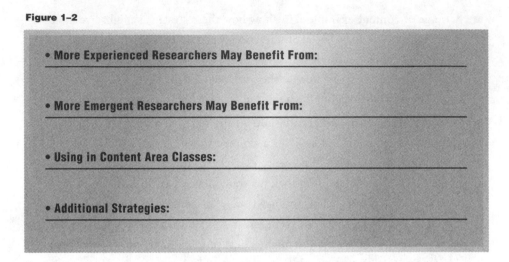

• **More Experienced Researchers May Benefit From:**

_____

• **More Emergent Researchers May Benefit From:**

_____

• **Using in Content Area Classes:**

_____

• **Additional Strategies:**

_____

an extension to each strategy that adds to the number of strategies you could choose from. The aim is not to be an exhaustive list, but instead to inspire your creation of further strategies.

■ **Discussion of the Common Core State Standards:** Throughout the book I aim to not just point you to standards, but help you understand the expectations they imply and to suggest teaching. Whenever a standard is discussed, see it as an invitation for you to reference your grade level's specific expectations and consider any revisions to the demonstration. This does not mean that you should only teach the standards; instead, use them as the endpoint and decide where on that road your students are currently standing.

■ **A chart in the Appendix for Common Core State Standards references:** "Looking Between the Standards and These Strategies: A Conversation" can help guide your students toward particular standards. When writing *Pathways to the Common Core: Accelerating Achievement* (2012) with Lucy Calkins and Mary Ehrenworth, we dove into an intensive study of the entire Common Core State Standards document, its development, and its implications. It was remarkable how talking, rereading, researching, and then doing it all again continued to uncover levels of nuance and points of connection. My hope is that the references throughout this book help you in your own study of these new expectations and serve as one part of that conversation.

A brief note about sources: Throughout this book I interchangeably use "sources" and "texts" to mean anything students can use to learn new information. I believe—and the Common Core State Standards echoes this—that students should learn to "read" a variety of sources, both print and digital, written words, images, video, interviews, and so on. It is a big world of information worth exploring.

Now, together we get to dive in to our own study and begin our own research on teaching research skills—considering methods to use, content to demonstrate, and planning for different types of studies. Expect that, like every research study, this one will be full of curiosity, false starts, retries, and new understandings. Even when things seem to not be going right, when students are doing those things that students sometimes do, consider that your research can serve as a model for their own studies. You can start a lesson by saying, "I've been studying something this month, something really important actually: I've been studying how what I say and think and do affects your learning. And more importantly, how what you say and think and do affects *my* learning." You are their most important example; your work sets the vision for theirs.

So, grab your notebook, a pen, maybe some colleagues, and let's go into your classroom together.

CHAPTER 2

No More Handouts

Teach Students to Narrow Down Topics and Evaluate Sources Independently

Research should be messy and exciting. Often one is armed with curiosity and a general direction. Right there in the term is the word "search," and from its earliest uses "research" was always used to not just describe *looking*, but really *investigating with great care* (OED online Dec. 2011). The term invites a driven, inquisitive mind, one that is trying to actively solve problems or gain new understandings. Are you buying a car? Having a baby? Wondering where the water from your faucet comes from? Or how languages spread across the globe? We progress through our life researching, seeking out answers to our questions, trying to find solutions to our struggles and fears. We do not always know which book is the best, which website to stick with, which personal advice will pan out. But we bravely forge ahead, taking right turns as well as wrong ones—getting stuck and then catching a lead that pushes us, with great momentum, ahead.

Teaching students to research, then, does not begin by assigning finite topics and handing out preselected sources. Instead it begins by embracing the uncertainty all of us feel when first researching a topic, then teaching budding researchers to do the things we have learned to do. For example, before our daughter was born and my wife and I first became parents, we collected a mile-high stack of books on pregnancy, babies, and parenting, not to mention the bookmarked websites and all the personal advice we could gather. We did not know what, exactly, we were looking for. We just knew: "We must learn about babies."

From the huge set of sources we decided that the best way to start is to just start, so we cracked open books, started surfing through sites. Through our research we learned which information was useful, which was not, which sources (and people) to listen to and which to avoid. For example, we got to the point where my wife refused to read anything on the Internet that I had not predetermined the anxiety-inducing level of. Some questions led to new questions and other searches; some ended up in dead-ends we knew weren't worth continuing down.

Even if someone had said, "Read these two books and then answer these six questions," there was a good chance those sources or those questions would not have been answers to questions we were still searching to find. The skills of research begin from the very first: "I must learn about . . ." We need to teach from that starting point and not jump too far down the line.

DEVELOPING HOW
Students Choose Topics and Gather Sources

The first link in the chain begins with how your students decide upon their topic and begin to gather sources. Sometimes in an effort to help students, some teachers assign a specific research topic, hand out sources, and even spell out what each paragraph of a final paper should contain. They do all of this because they want to get students to "the real work" of research projects: note-taking and writing about the topic. Unfortunately, when we are the ones rushing students ahead, engagement drops dramatically as we take the intellectual rigor out of the job. Probably half of the work of research is just figuring out what you want to say and who or what will help you say it. Taking this out of the equation is removing some of the most important work. The Common Core State Standards expect that all students, beginning in fourth grade, are able to gather information from multiple print and digital sources—*independently* (writing standard 8). Better for them to start practicing with you now than waiting for the new standardized tests, or later trouble with high school or college work, to let you know what they can and cannot do alone.

Additionally, handing students topics and preselected sources removes a natural and important step of learning to do anything: making errors. If we are developing students to be creative, flexible, independent learners, then we cannot scrub away opportunities for mistakes to be made and corrections to be learned. Often times we learn more from what did not go well and we have learned to fix.

There is one more critical point to consider in regard to the sources our students choose. No matter how well executed a lesson, how engaging and clear, if students cannot read the texts they have in their hands they simply cannot apply your teaching. Just sit next to any student who generally seems to have difficulty not completing class work or homework and ask them to read out loud a small bit of the texts they have been "reading." In many cases that lack of productivity is not just laziness; it's often a sign of real struggle. Education researcher Richard Allington even titled an article on content-area reading with a quote from a consistently struggling high school student: "You Can't Learn Much from Books You Can't Read" (*Education Leadership* 2002, pp. 16–19). In the article he writes: "The idea of harder textbooks has captured the attention of educators and policymakers interested in raising academic achievement. But harder books won't foster the growth of content learning. Think about your own attempts to acquire new content knowledge. Imagine you want to learn about building a website. Do you reject many of the books you might use because they are too easy? Do you say to yourself, 'Gosh, only 11 words on this page that I can't pronounce—not hard enough for me!'" So, do open up a wider net of sources for your students, being vigilant that what they choose they are able to actually use. (See "But What if They Want to Research Unicorns or the Cure for Baldness?: Teach Students to Let Available Sources Select What Is Possible to Study" for more on choosing sources.)

Whether you are a Social Studies teacher using some of these strategies and methods as your students spend a day or two reading texts on the Civil War, or an English Language Arts teacher beginning a unit on research reading and writing in which they may be reading texts for a week or more before moving to writing, we need to equip students with the tools to dive bravely and carefully into any new content that comes their way.

Here, for example, is how you might differentiate support for your students in gathering sources. Consider their level of familiarity with the topic being researched, the breadth or focus you will teach them to have, where they get their sources, and how you will teach them to use them.

Differentiating Instruction for Gathering Topics and Sources

Teaching for more emergent researchers	Teach students to study topics they are already familiar with, drawing on both personal experience and sources for their study. Help them gather and use materials that have clear main-idea-and-details structure, with vocabulary clearly supported, most likely starting within sets you have created.	Teach students to select topics that interest them and ways to choose a segment of that topic to study. Support them in selecting sources, including library and Internet searches. Teach them to start with accessible texts before moving to more complicated ones for skimming and fact-checking.	Teach students to develop a focus within a topic, which they can continue to narrow or change over time. Show them how to choose most sources through library and Internet searches, flexibly moving between more and less complex texts, matching how they use the text (e.g., read, skim) to its readability. **Teaching for more experienced researchers**

▶ **Investigation Starts with "I":** Teach Students to Find Their Own Research Topics—Because They Will Have to Eventually

Teach your students a range of strategies for gathering many potential topics, so later they can evaluate and choose between them. One strategy is to start with prior knowledge, listing topics they know a lot, some, and only a little about.

It helps our learners if we break complex, abstract tasks (like coming up with compelling research topics) into smaller steps that are more easily replicable. Then, as they become more proficient and automatic, we can take those strategies away. In other words, you may teach students to make a chart, like the one I describe below, until they become so good at it that they can do that thinking internally. It is the pedagogical concept of "scaffolding." Of course, this means they cannot only do a strategy once; it is repetition that allows for scaffolding to be removed. Luckily, the Common Core State Standards expect that students will undertake not just long research projects, but also brief, fast bouts of research many times throughout the year (writing standard 7). Chapter 7 suggests ways to build in this level of repetition and quick practice throughout the school year.

Teach students to begin with an analysis of their own expertise, allowing each area to spark other potential topics. One version of this is to make a three-column chart: list topics you know a lot about in the first, topics you know some about in the second, and topics you do not know much about but would like to learn in the third. Once students amass several, teach them to choose a few to jot a couple paragraphs about, testing out their knowledge.

When demonstrating this strategy for a sixth-grade class I could say:

> "Writers start with what they know best first, then they go from there. The same is true for great researchers—scientists, historians, journalists, authors—anyone who makes research a part of their lives begins with what they know. A scientist trying to find a cure begins with everything that is already known before starting out on a new quest for answers.

> "One way to do this is to ask yourself, 'What am I an expert in already?' and then use that to brainstorm a bunch of other topics you could research. I made a fast chart in my notebook with three columns and labeled them 'topic I know a lot about,' 'some about,' and 'not much about.' Watch how I use this to help me brainstorm.

> "I know a lot about cooking, or at least how to make some meals really well. So I could put 'cooking' in this first column. Now, if I keep that idea in mind, I feel like I can jump right over to this middle column and jot down 'baking' because I know *something* about that, but am also pretty terrible at it. I usually burn cookies or they turn out too thin. Which leads me right to this last column. I realize I don't know much about *why* things mix to make food great or terrible, to make cookies rise or lie flat and just burn. So I could put 'the chemistry of cooking and baking' in this last column. I also could put, 'where food comes from' in the second column, because I know a little bit about this from what I have seen on TV, but I feel like I could really research more.

> "Okay, I am going to freeze here for a second. Did you notice how I started in one column but then I didn't just stop there? I held onto the ideas I was working with a bit longer and used them to jump from column to column and back again. Once I run out of steam with one idea I can begin a new one. I can think of things I like to do, things I see around, things I have heard in the news, things I am learning in Science or Social Studies. My goal is to fill this list up with many different ideas as quickly as I can. Once I have made a sizable list, I can begin free-writing about any of the topics I jotted. Not whole entire essays, just lots of little paragraphs about different topics to really see how much I know and what more I want to know. Watch quickly how I do that . . ."

That last bit there, where I stopped to put into words what I had just done, is crucial to helping our students develop learning *habits* that can become internalized, not just enact *assignments* that are later forgotten. To help our students transfer what we are teaching into their own practice, we need to ensure that we are as explicit and clear in our teaching as possible. Having a balance between demonstrating a strategy and explaining the parts of it helps to achieve just this. Any effective lesson will have a teacher both doing and explaining.

When Murshea tried this strategy she filled her list very quickly, then picked one to write briefly about on the following page, then another from her brainstorming, and so on. (See Figure 2–1.)

At the end of a lesson like this I will often say that this same habit can be accomplished without the three columns, that students can choose to make columns or little paragraphs or bulleted lists or some other way of organizing their ideas. The goal is the thinking involved, not the perfect enactment of the strategy I showed.

Figure 2–1 Murshea's Listing and Longer Writing Entries

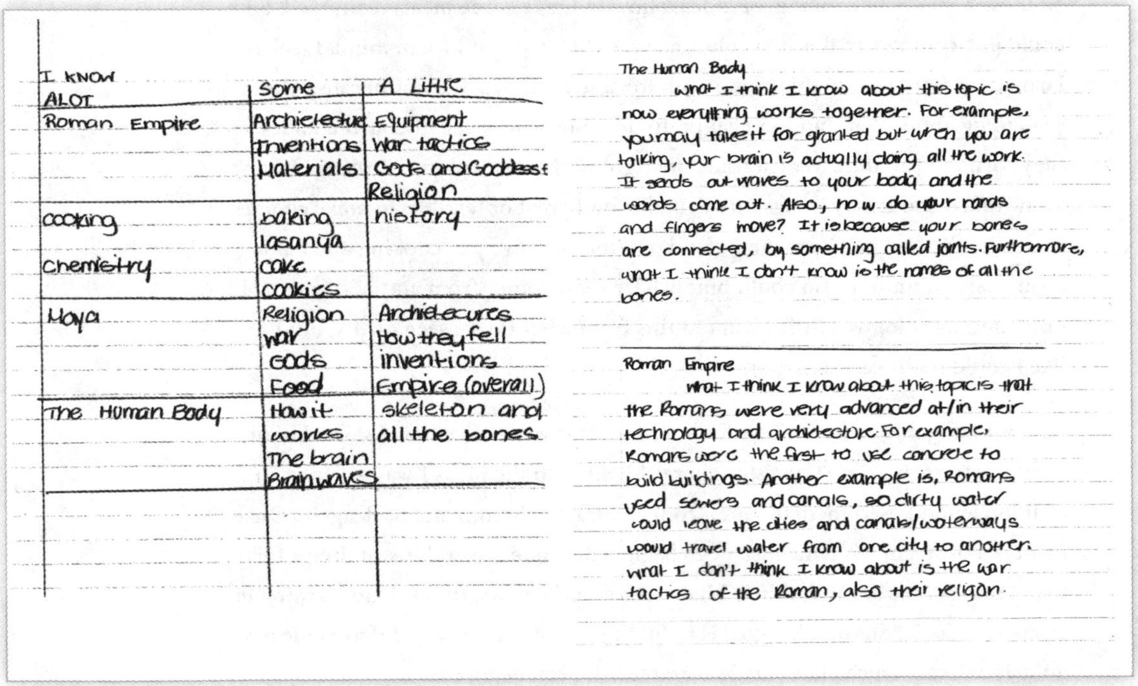

I know ALOT	Some	A Little
Roman Empire	Archietecture Inventions Materials	Equipment War tactics Gods and Goddesses Religion
cooking chemistry	baking lasanya cake cookies	history
Maya	Religion war Gods Food	Archietecures How they fell inventions Empire (overall)
The Human Body	How it works The brain Brainwaves	skeleton and all the bones

The Human Body

what I think I know about this topic is how everything works together. For example, you may take it for granted but when you are talking, your brain is actually doing all the work. It sends out waves to your body and the words come out. Also, how do your hands and fingers move? It is because your bones are connected, by something called joints. Furthermore, what I think I don't know is the names of all the bones.

Roman Empire

what I think I know about this topic is that the Romans were very advanced at/in their technology and archidectore. For example, Romans were the first to use concrete to build buildings. Another example is, Romans used sewers and canals, so dirty water could leave the cities and canals/waterways would travel water from one city to another. what I don't think I know about is the war tactics of the Roman, also their religon.

DEVISING TEACHING THAT MATCHES YOUR STUDENTS

• More Experienced Researchers May Benefit From:

More experienced researchers could be taught to not just write from topics, but to narrow them. This strategy could be varied by stopping after jotting a few topics, then choosing one topic to lift onto a new page and repeating the same three columns, only this time for narrowed versions of that topic—again, with the goal of collecting many, many potential topics. So "where food comes from" could go at the top of a page and be narrowed down and written within those columns: "how eggs are gathered and sold," "where meat in the supermarket comes from," "how chemicals (that I can't pronounce) on food labels are made and why."

• More Emergent Researchers May Benefit From:

More emergent researchers tend to begin with large topics. Time and teaching can help them narrow them more. For students that may find this strategy complicated, fight the urge to assign them topics and instead forgo the multiple columns. Students can list topics they feel they are already somewhat expert in or would like to be expert in and go straight to writing a little bit about each to explore their thinking.

• Using in Content-Area Classes:

In a content-area study, you may decide to begin by providing students with an "umbrella" topic (say, the Civil War) and giving them a bit of introduction. Some brief video clips, a general lecture, looking at period artwork, or looking at collections of primary sources can give students just enough background knowledge to make educated choices about topics, without having to study too much up front. Then have students use the above strategy: "What I know a lot about [the Civil War], some about [the Civil War], not much but would like to know more about . . ." And then again write longer entries trying these out.

• Additional Strategies:

On any day of collecting, teach students to move very quickly from listing to writing longer thinking entries. These are a bit like conversations with oneself, testing out how much a writer knows and needs to learn as well as seeing how interested he or she is in potential topics. Teach students to write about both what they already know and what they hope to learn, perhaps using phrases like, "What I think I know is . . ." and "I am not as sure about . . ." or "I really want to find out . . ."

▶ But What If They Want to Research Unicorns or the Cure for Baldness?: Teach Students to Let Available Sources Select What Is Possible to Study

Teach students to narrow down their topic ideas. One important strategy is to look for available sources and allow their number and their readability to narrow down and refine topic choices.

After even just a class period or two of collecting potential topics, the number of ideas swirling around the room can feel both exciting and a bit intimidating. Of course you could have every student turn in a card with their topics written down so you can cross off the pie-in-the-sky ones and circle the topic you know will produce the best outcome. However, this would again scrub away the chance for students to learn how to do this kind of evaluation for themselves. Additionally, it would erase for you the chance to see what they do when left to their own devices. Their successes and flops help you in your role as personal trainer, deciding which strategies will develop their research independence.

One strategy for narrowing down topics is to let sources be a guide. With a visit to a library, searching digital sources, or even looking through bins of books and articles in your classroom, our researchers can learn to cross out those pies-in-the-sky before we have to.

If you schedule a visit to your school or public library, first, have your students narrow down their listed topics to the top three or four and go with those in mind. Teach them to choose those they feel the most compelled to study, and even more importantly, believe they will find the most information on. Once there and before they rush to grab books off the shelves, teach them to evaluate each potential topic by looking at how many sources are available for each. Sometimes, you will need to teach them to widen or focus topics in order to find sources. With a class of fifth graders you might say:

> "Sometimes researchers just can't learn what they hope to learn, because there aren't any materials on that subject, or there aren't the right instruments to use, or the knowledge they would need to gather just isn't available yet. So they are limited by what is currently known, what sources are available. This leads them to refine their first plans.

> "So today, we are going to let the books available help us narrow down our topics. To start, don't pick up every book you see. Instead, first look to see how many

books exist on *each* topic you brought with you. Then consider, from what is available, which topic you will be able to learn the most about. Watch me for a moment while I try this:

> "I have three topics that I want to check on—where does food I buy at the store come from, what was the first ancient bird, and I want to learn about the American Revolution because I'm studying that in Social Studies. Watch as I walk over to each of those sections to see what is available. If I find a lot of books on the American Revolution and very few on cooking, I might decide to go with the Revolution topic. Let's see . . ."

After you let your class loose, predictably, within the first several minutes of the library visit you will want to call your class back together. Some will have found a topic with a bunch of books; some will not but will naturally refine their topic or change it just enough to expand their search. Still others will just feel stuck. For example, one year I was working with a fifth-grade team at a school in Queens, New York. On our library visit day I was talking with one student, Dominique, who had trouble finding books that matched her topic. After talking with her, I thought her experience would help the entire class, so I gathered them together and taught them to refine their search before giving up on their topic. I used Dominique's example (though I made sure when I talked about her I highlighted what she had learned to do, rather than make it look like she had done something wrong):

> "Dominique just did something really smart that I wanted to share with all of you. She was looking for books on one of her topics, 'kids' games in the Dominican Republic,' and she couldn't find any. Instead of just giving up on the topic, because it really interested her, we talked about maybe first revising the topic she was searching for. I suggested—and I think all of you could do this too—that she ask herself if there is a larger category her topic could fit inside of, or, if it was already big, were there smaller topics that could fit underneath?

> "Dominique thought kids' games in the Dominican Republic could be both big and small. If it were big, it could have small categories like maybe 'checkers, dominoes, and soccer.' It also could fit inside of larger categories like 'life in the Dominican Republic' or 'people in the Caribbean' or 'kids games.' She thought about all of these and realized that she liked the larger category options; they were more interesting to her. And you know what? When she went back to the shelf she found two books on the Dominican Republic and a bunch of others on life in other Caribbean countries.

"So, if you find yourself getting stuck for books—and later when you look on-line for articles and websites—first stop and ask yourself if your topic could have larger or small categories."

Using the actual available sources not only can teach students to find the most profitable topic for their research, it also can provide a concrete way of looking for broader or narrower topics.

DEVISING TEACHING THAT MATCHES YOUR STUDENTS

• More Experienced Researchers May Benefit From:

Experienced researchers will benefit from learning how to search the library independently, both physically and electronically. Invite your library/media specialist to talk briefly about the Dewey Decimal system of organization, showing students that with topics in mind they can already chart a path around the book collection. Show them that they can then plot their course before actually getting up to look.

• More Emergent Researchers May Benefit From:

Teach students to judge up front which sources are most useful to them at the beginning, middle, and end of their research reading. Show students how to make a plan for digging into the topic, deciding how to progress across the materials they have gathered. I will often suggest that students put sticky notes on the front of their books labeled with phrases like "start with this" (for books they feel they can read fluently and will provide the most general overview of important concepts and topics), "read later" (for ones that they will need some background knowledge on first), "good for skimming" (for ones that either feel very complicated or perhaps very specific in scope, useful for pulling out important information but difficult to read from cover to cover).

• Using in Content-Area Classes:

Most science trade books offer cover-to-cover coverage of a topic (such as, everything about "electricity") and often Social Studies books do the same, often in a mix of expository and literary nonfiction ("the revolutionary war" told through anecdotes and facts). Teach students to also use the table of contents and the index to see if the part of the larger whole they are interested in is handled by that text. Just because the book title is Civil War does not mean it will talk about "childhood during . . ."

• Additional Strategies:

Teach students that researchers walk around day in and day out with their topic swimming inside their minds, looking for new information and interesting connections. Help them see that sources need not always be print—that Internet videos, television shows, activities they do in class or at home, even interviews are all additional and very valuable sources. Plan to support students in getting as much as they can from these additional sources. For instance, you may decide to teach a few interview strategies, like how a good journalist will always try to ask one or two follow-up questions. Or perhaps you will demonstrate how to search the television guide for channels and shows that could add to students' topics, like the History Channel or Animal Planet. Certainly if you engage your students in an activity in class, like a science experiment, you will want to highlight that connection as well.

▶ I Feel Like We Have Met Somewhere Before:
Teach Students to Find a Unique Focus for Their Research by Considering Their Audience

Teach students to consider their potential audience and use those imagined readers to guide their research process. One way to do this is to write brief entries considering what you assume your readers do not already know and what you have to research to support their learning.

If students are researching merely because it is an assignment, then their engagement with the process and their learning will only be a fraction of what it could be. Think about the moments you have researched in your life. When a friend had a new baby on the way, the audience for your research was those new parents, and you looked for books to buy for them that matched their personality and needs. If you became passionately involved in a cause, you may have conducted research to help you convince politicians or write a letter to an editor. If you were contemplating a big career change or move to a new city, the research audience may have been you yourself, and all of your hopes and trepidations came into account as you chose sources. It is essential, then, to have our students begin to consider their audiences now, as imagined readers will affect not just what they write later but also what they collect and consider now.

In *Assessing Writers* (2005) Carl Anderson writes, "Students tell me time after time that they are writing for 'the class.' While the class is a perfectly good audience, I want children to learn that they can write pieces for specific individuals in the class (friends or classmates with similar interests) or outside the class (relatives or community leaders) and also for a more general audience (readers of the school or local newspaper)" (p. 44). Anderson explains that people generally initiate writing because they have a real audience in mind, and if our students want to be truly independent writers, then they need to do the same.

One strategy is to teach students to write brief entries in which they consider what their readers may not already know and what they will need to research to fill those holes. When demonstrating for a seventh-grade class I could say:

> "When we research we often do so in order to teach ourselves or others something new. Sometimes in school, though, we feel like research is just an assignment to be completed, something that only 'your class' or 'your teacher' will care about. I would like us to treat this study differently, to make our study matter and be important beyond just this classroom.
>
> "So an important place to start is to ask yourself, 'What do I think people who might learn from my research may not already know?' and then, 'What will I have to find out so I can be sure they learn about those parts of this topic?' Watch how I try this with the topic I am studying, the solar system. Let me first think before I write . . . I think people that learn from my research may not already know . . . well, I actually think most people know how many planets there are and the order they are in. So, I guess I don't need to spend too much time studying those obvious facts. . . . But, they probably won't know what the planets are made of, at least not specifically. And more importantly, how what the planets are composed of is so different from one planet to another . . . so that means I would have to research the chemical makeup of the planets and start comparing them to each other . . .
>
> "Do you see what I'm doing? I'm taking a moment, very early on in collecting sources and starting to read, to think about my audience and what they might need to know. It is helping me focus or narrow my research, so I spend time learning those things that I think readers will most need to learn."

Harmukh wrote an entry where he considered what his audience would need to know. He did not just think of information they were lacking but also their feelings or attitudes toward the topic and how he hoped his research could affect or change them. (See Figure 2–2.)

From this entry you can sense how much more focused his search for sources and information will be, but you can also hear how passionately he is engaging with his topic. He has a real sense of purpose now, not just an assignment to complete.

Figure 2–2 Harmukh's Audience Brainstorming Entry

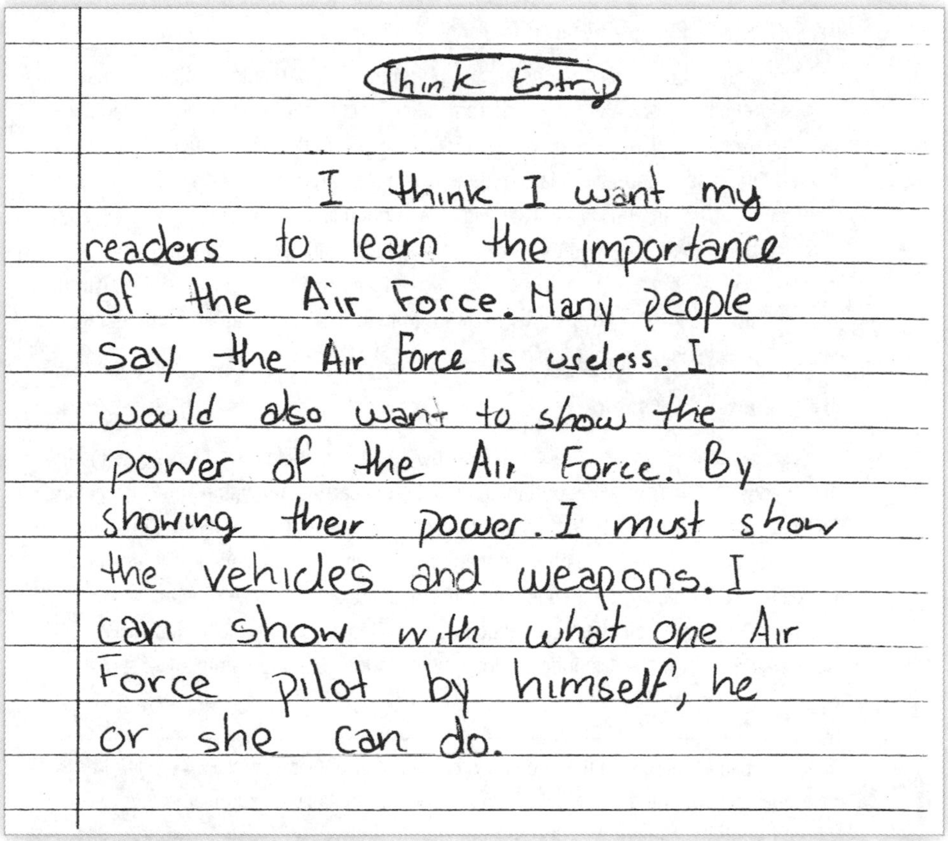

(Think Entry)

> I think I want my readers to learn the importance of the Air Force. Many people say the Air Force is useless. I would also want to show the power of the Air Force. By showing their power. I must show the vehicles and weapons. I can show with what one Air Force pilot by himself, he or she can do.

DEVISING TEACHING THAT MATCHES YOUR STUDENTS

• More Experienced Researchers May Benefit From:

More experienced researchers could be introduced to a strategy in the best-selling book for college and adult researchers, *The Craft of Research* (2008), in which the authors suggest trying out active verbs within potential research topics. Teach students to write out a sentence like "I want to find out about . . ." and then instead of simply writing a topic, "chimpanzees," make a full sentence that contains a verb like "contributes," "conflicts," or "develops." The idea is that richer research topics consider something active, like how one part of a topic "contributed to" a larger part, or how one part "developed" into something else. So a potential research statement could sound like: "I want to find out about how chimpanzees in the wild contributed to the study of humans."

* More Emergent Researchers May Benefit From:

More emergent researchers can be taught to first plan for particular audiences, just as that quote from Carl Anderson was suggesting. It may seem like a minor exercise, but pays tremendous dividends. Teach students to assign themselves very specific readers, perhaps in addition to larger audiences if they are really set on that as well. Choosing "I'm writing this with my friend Kyle in mind and other fourth graders" leads students to collect sources, choose information, and even write with the very particular needs of that person in mind. In turn it leads to a more purposeful research process. Just be sure to have students return to this person over and over by doing so with your own choice in your lessons.

* Using in Content-Area Classes:

In a content-area study, the direction of narrowing a topic could be a bit more defined. Teach your students the kinds of thinking most often carried out within your discipline. For instance, in the study of historical figures, there may be fruitful research in looking at how that person's early life affected them, or what other figures' ideas influenced his/her own. In science, as so much is interconnected, looking at a phenomenon within a larger system can potentially help students find an interesting topic, or looking at debates that exist in the scientific community can often be a good jumping-off point.

* Additional Strategies:

Students can assume who the audiences could be for their research, which would be a fine start, or you could teach them to research this as well, to discover just who particular audiences may be. One way to do this is to locate issues attached to their topics. You can for instance teach students to search the Internet for terms like "petition," "conserve," or "save." Typing "petition" and "sharks," for example, reveals several active groups involved in causes like stopping shark finning or protecting other species. Another is to keep your eyes open for types of experts and specific organizations quoted within sources and then research those—for instance, noting that someone quoted is called an "astrophysicist" and then finding out what such a person does. Again, this has the effect of helping students not just learn more about the world of their topic, but also narrowing down their topic.

DEVELOPING HOW
Students Evaluate Sources

The Common Core State Standards place a focus on students being able to evaluate sources and information. Fourth and fifth graders, they expect, should draw on "relevant information" in their research to prepare them for being middle school and high school students who can also assess the "credibility and accuracy" of sources that information comes from (writing standard 8). The purpose for this seems tremendously clear: it creates more cautious and careful consumers and citizens. Instead of taking an infomercial's claims of "tighter abs in thirty days, just by sitting!" at face value or listening to competing politicians argue polar-opposite claims, our students could potentially live their lives with the same thoughtful and open eyes that they have through the process of research.

Now ask yourself, "Do I ever, really, ask my students to evaluate their sources?" In most classrooms—including my own—it could be quite rare. We hand them what we hand them, and both they and we take them at face value. A seventh grader once said to me, when asked if he thought everything he was reading was true, "Well, it's in a book, isn't it?"

The need for students to have a range of strategies to draw on is made even clearer when teaching them to evaluate sources. There is no one way to know if a source is right for what you are trying to say, no one magic test to signal whether this particular article is accurate and relevant. It takes a trained eye, with a bunch of little "tests" to run, to find the most useful and most accurate information. What needs to go on in our students' minds is a bit like a page from a dog-eared medical book on a shelf in my parents' bedroom. In *Taking Care of Your Child: A Parent's Guide to Medical Care* (1977), each section lists potential childhood ailments, along with a flow-chart of questions and answers intended to calm the nerves of worried parents and help them provide proper care for their woeful child. The page on "Fever" has a flow-chart with this text:

> *Is the child less than four months of age? Yes—See physician now; No—Is there stiffness of the neck, confusion, marked irritability, lethargy . . . ? Yes— See physician now; No—Has the fever lasted more than 24 hours?*

We need to support our students in having these same sorts of flow-charts for assessing accuracy, moving from one test of relevancy and accuracy to the next. Of course, the level of each student's sophistication will be determined by how long and nuanced these internal checklists are.

Here, for example, is how you might think about supporting your students in evaluating sources, adjusting the level and amount of your support based on their development. In this case, it means teaching tried-and-true rules of thumb, noticing overtly opinionated pieces (as those will be the easiest to learn these skills from), and considering texts within and against a larger body of knowledge.

Differentiating Instruction for Evaluating Sources

Help students follow a few rules-of-thumb for checking the reliability of sources, like "check the publication date" and "choose websites from colleges, and familiar organizations (like PBS)."	Teach students to read asking themselves, "Is this text more informational or more opinion based?" They will most likely have greater ease in evaluating opinion pieces. Teach them, then, to notice when a claim is made and check if support is given or when support is lacking. Help them carry this to video and eventually to expository texts as well.	Show students how to evaluate sources in comparison to one another, noticing when contradictions arise. Teach them to determine if the conflicts are based on point of view or serious inaccuracies. Additionally, teach them to do "background checks," to research individuals' or organizations' potential biases.	**Teaching for more experienced researchers**

Teaching for more emergent researchers

▶ I Know Because Your Voice Goes Up a Little When You Lie: Teach Students to Look for Signs of an Opinion Being Passed Off as a Fact

Teach students ways to evaluate an author's claims. One is to look backward (and when needed read forward) to see if the author's ideas are clearly supported and described for readers or if they appear weak or missing.

Concrete, memorable images often help make abstract ideas stick with our students. When talking with students about evaluating the claims made within their sources, I will often speak of it as if authors are building a path of stones from you, the reader, to their idea. Careful and thoughtful reading (or viewing) involves pausing when you notice an idea is being stated and then going back to see if you can find the stepping stones the author left for you. Stopping at the point of an idea to look at how it was supported is work the Common Core expects of students in elementary school: "explain how an author uses reasons and evidence to support particular points in a text." In middle and high school, then, it is also necessary to step back, look at that path, and evaluate how sturdy and substantial those stones appear: ". . . assessing whether the reasoning is sound and the evidence is relevant and sufficient to support the claims" (reading standard 8). The metaphor is great because you can easily say, "Would you feel safe walking across those very few, small, slightly cracked rocks?"

When demonstrating this, I often choose to start with a text that is obvious in its flaws—the lesson is the time for all of us to "get it"; the first introduction should not be so challenging that it is hard to decipher. Perhaps you find a text or you write one yourself, like this one I wrote for a demonstration with sixth graders:

> *Cuttlefish live in the ocean. They look a great deal like squid with their long tentacles and a large "head," called the mantle. They eat crabs and fish and sometimes small shrimp, which they hunt, often by sneaking up on their prey by first camouflaging themselves. Perhaps no ocean creature is as unique as the cuttlefish. It uses the suction cups on its tentacles to grab the prey and pull it to its mouth.*

With this text I can now teach students to stop when they hear an opinion, what the Common Core State Standards seem to refer to interchangeably as "points," "arguments," or "claims" of an author. Then, either in writing or in their minds, hold that claim and go backward to find the stepping stones that lead up to it. In this instance I could read this little paragraph and then stop at the opinion and jot it down:

> *Perhaps no ocean creature is as unique as the cuttlefish.*

Then say:

> "Now that I've found a sentence that feels like an opinion, I'm going to try to figure out if the author is building a path for us to walk on—from us to this idea. If this idea is really well supported, then there should be a bunch of really solid stones laid out for us to walk across; each fact is another great big stone. We can back up and reread and also read forward a bit to see how many stones there are—the facts—and how sturdy they are—how well they connect to this idea.

> "Let's go back and make a quick map of those stones—I'm going to jot them down so we can talk about them, but I could also just do this quickly in my mind. Let's try it, first sentence: 'Cuttlefish live in the ocean.' Is that a fact that connects in any way to this idea, that no ocean creature is as unique? Mmm, maybe . . . I guess so. It is letting us know they live in the ocean. Okay, I'll add that stone to our path.

> "Now the next sentence: 'They look a great deal like squid.' Does that get me closer to knowing they are more unique than any other ocean creature? Well, it

is about ocean creatures, but is it a fact that supports them being very unique? Mmm, not really; in fact it says they are a lot alike. Though just because they look like a squid doesn't mean they are completely like them . . . maybe we will write it down, but I'll draw it a little bit smaller than the first one. Let's keep reading . . ."

I demonstrate this thinking and then invite students to talk with a partner briefly, considering the other sentences. I now have a chart like the one shown in Figure 2–3.

Figure 2–3 Stepping Stones Chart

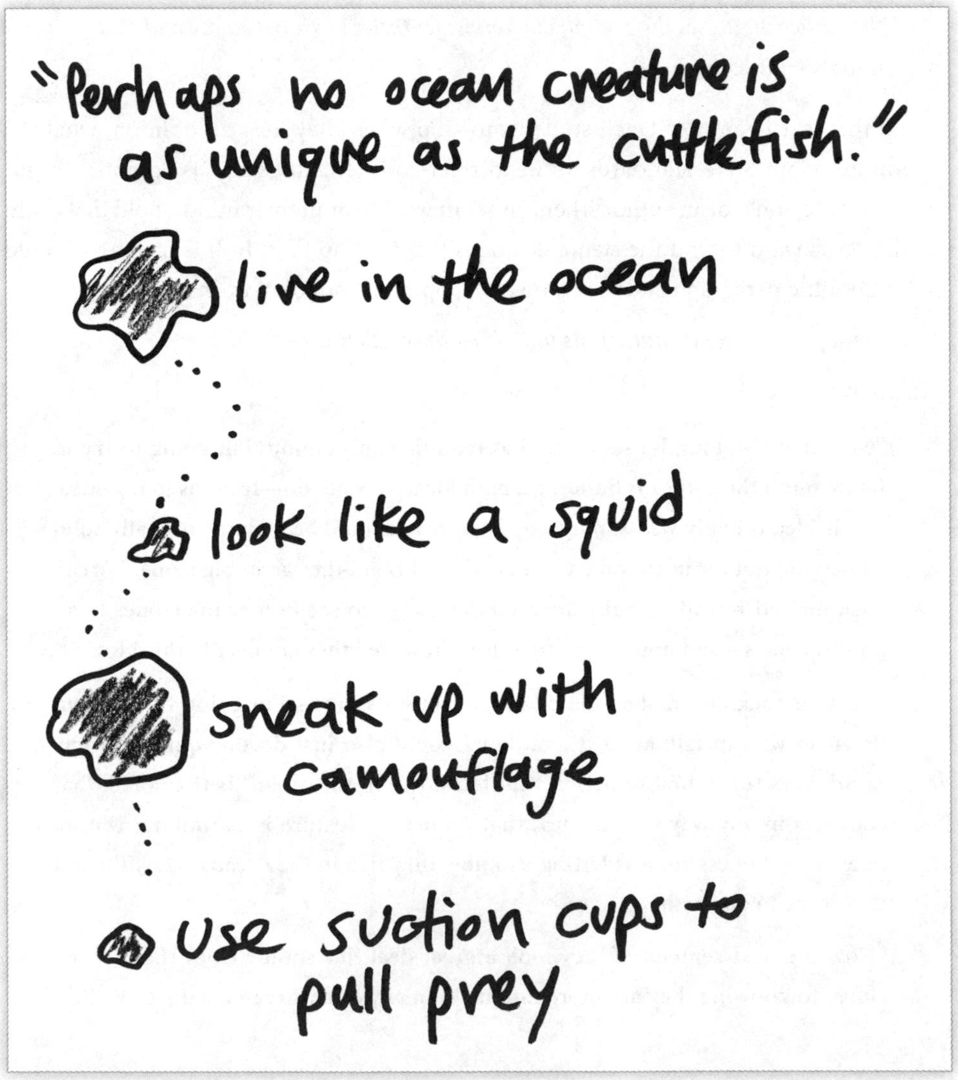

This is where the expectations of the Common Core State Standards stop for elementary school students; being able to look at claims and trace an author's evidence is described as fifth-grade level work. This does not mean we must stop here; in fact, it's not a stretch for upper elementary students to consider how substantially those bits of evidence support the author's idea. Next, I can say to the class:

> "Now that we have a path laid out, let's go back and ask ourselves, could we walk across those stones to get to that idea? Do they feel strong enough to support us? If we can't safely get across, then we know this author did not support this idea enough. We know we may not be able to believe it just from this one person and this one source. We would have to go to other sources to make sure this idea is really true.
>
> "Okay, let's try it. Looking across the stones in our path, does it seem like there are enough, and is each strong enough, to get us across? Tell your partner what you think and which stones are making you feel like the idea is well supported or not."

The metaphor is helpful, because it is both engaging and helps to turn an abstract concept into one that is a bit more concrete. For your own classroom, use whatever metaphor or language will be most familiar to your students.

DEVISING TEACHING THAT MATCHES YOUR STUDENTS

• More Experienced Researchers May Benefit From:

More experienced researchers can look for patterns across sources covering the same topic. Any break in the pattern invites further analysis—for instance, if three books on sharks all talk about their habitats, their hunting patterns, and their life cycle. Then one has a whole section on saving sharks because they are misunderstood. Teach readers to stop and analyze the accuracy of that viewpoint. A deviation, as in this example, does not mean the text is necessarily wrong; instead it just means a reader should activate their internal flow-chart to check reliability.

• More Emergent Researchers May Benefit From:

More emergent researchers will benefit from learning general rules of thumb for checking the reliability and accuracy of sources, like checking for a recent publication date. For online sources, Harvey Daniels and Stephanie Harvey's book *Comprehension and Collaboration: Inquiry Circles in Action* (2009), has a section on finding reliable Internet information. You might look to their book or to your own library/media specialist for the latest thinking on this constantly changing topic. For instance, the rule of thumb about steering students toward websites that end in ".org" or ".edu" as being the most reliable is changing as we speak. Now anyone, even you or I, can purchase an ".org" address without actually having an organization.

• Using in Content-Area Classes:

Primary sources become an interesting consideration, especially in a Social Studies classroom. This does not necessarily mean checking on how authentic they are—that feels like more graduate-level work—but instead considering the point of view or bias presented within them. We need to teach our students to hold the context of primary documents in mind while reading them. Just because a writer says leeches cure all disease does not make it automatically true.

• Additional Strategies:

Students can also be taught to perform secret-agent-style "background checks," hunting for less-obvious information. One way is to research the author or publisher of information to find out their background and if they have a particular point of view or even a deeper bias. Often this is more fruitful for online or video sources, though it could be practiced on many sources. Another way is to question if there are points of view or sides missing from the sources they have collected so far, for example, are there people saying sharks are actually quite dangerous and should be feared more than protected? Or is Britain's point of view during the American Revolution written about?

Reflecting on Student Growth

Take stock of your students' practices with narrowing down topics and evaluating sources both before and after you have taught some strategies and given them time to practice. Aim for your teaching to increase both the *quantity* of strategies they know and the *quality* with which they develop topics and select sources.

To assess quantity, notice times when students get a bit stuck. Students who have limited ways to gather and narrow topics, for instance, will often jot an idea or two and then drift away—either staring out the window or into a distracting conversation. This is an indication that the student needs to learn more ways of working and have more time to practice each. Ask yourself:

- Which strategies have I taught this student? How many different approaches to this skill does he/she know?

- How much *repeated* practice have they had with any one strategy? Have they just collected one topic and stopped? Could I suggest they try to gather a few others and in the end choose the best?

To assess quality, look at students' behavior—as with quantity—but also consider their work within a progression of sophistication. Is their work rigorous enough for the grade level? It helps to not just think about your school or district, but to picture all students in the entire country in your students' grade level. How would their work stack up? Ask yourself:

- If this student is distracted easily, is it because they are either having difficulty or they find the task too easy? Is there a new strategy (or a variation to the one they are having trouble with) that I could share with them?

- Compared to the Common Core State Standards from this grade level, how are students beginning to compare to the expectations of both the "Research to Build Knowledge and Present Knowledge" strand from the writing standards and the "Integration of Knowledge and Ideas" strand of the reading standards?

- When I look at the progressions presented in this chapter (see pages 12 and 24), is this student moving up and ready for additional, more advanced kinds of research teaching?

With the help of your careful eye and expert guidance, your students can move away from overly orchestrated topics and preselected texts and enter into a more exciting, more authentic research experience.

CHAPTER 3

Stop the Random Numbers and Recopied Paragraphs

Teach Students to Note-Take with Purpose, Not Indifference

Note-taking feels synonymous with nonfiction reading. It is collegiate, professional, like there is a job to do and notes will help get it done. It brings to mind those movie scenes of an undergraduate student hunched over stacks of books, feverishly reading and scribbling notes underneath the green-glass library lamps and large stained-glass windows of an unspecified Ivy League university. The more he reads and jots, the closer he'll get to that triumphant movie climax when he passes the exam or makes the discovery or outwits the stringent professor. I think we all dream a bit while teaching a note-taking lesson, that one day all of our students will be in that exact role.

They, however, often do not see it this way. Instead, note-taking becomes a redundant end in itself. They take notes to, well, just take notes—page upon page of teeny little details, long shopping lists of facts, with little organization or thought. Later when looking back (if they ever look back) those numbers and lists and plagiarized sections of text just hang out in the space of their notebook, "1863?" "4,000 pounds?" "The migration of the monarch is as heroic as it is mundane?" What does any of that mean? When you ask a student *why* she wrote a particular thing down, instead of giving a movie script response, she will often say, "Well, because it's *a fact*." Insert: "Duh."

This chapter is built around considering better alternatives to that *why*. Why do we take notes? Surely we all do it so differently in our adult lives, and use those notes in different ways after. I, for instance, take copious notes, but rarely review them later. My note-taking while reading or while listening helps me organize my thinking and stores it in my mental bank. I am usually, then, very good at recalling or at least remembering where to go back to double-check. I have some friends who write down almost nothing, but then rely heavily on those few essential notes. Still others write volumes and refer to them, pore over them, talk to others about them.

What all of our adult experiences with note-taking have in common is not the *type* of notes, but the reason why we do it. We take notes to develop expertise—to know more about that subject than before we read, watched, or heard about it. It is not the kind of notes that matters, but the practice of using notes to gather key points, to help us remember and return to different sources of information later, to help us put more ideas into our busy minds.

If note-taking, then, is really about learning, consider the difference between a novice on a topic and an expert. At the Reading and Writing Project we have grappled with how to engage students in reading and learning from nonfiction sources and came to find that suggesting students think of themselves as budding *experts*, not just reading for the sake of reading, often led to greater engagement and more thoughtful reading. This led me to wonder: so, just what is an expert? In *How People Learn: Brain, Mind, Experience, and School* (National Academy of Sciences 2000), there's a chapter titled "How Experts Differ from Novices." Citing research on this topic, the authors explain that experts not only know a lot of facts about their subject, they are also able to group these facts in a meaningful way—noticing patterns or themes—and they can apply these patterns in a variety of settings. For instance, historians David Starkey and Alison Weir did not just know reams of facts about Queen Elizabeth I in order to write acclaimed biographies about that famous Tudor, they also understood important themes about her life and her time period, and when they needed to apply that knowledge to less-documented bits of her life they filled in the holes with extremely well-educated guesses. They are experts because they have a lot of knowledge, have digested it, and are able to apply it. In *Pathways to the Common Core: Accelerating Achievement* (2012), we write about how the Common Core State Standards interestingly appear to follow a progression of "expert building." Experts need facts. Compare this to the informational writing standards that expect first graders to "supply some facts about the topic." Experts can see patterns and concepts that link facts together, and the standards require fifth graders to "group related information logically." Experts are able to apply concepts to a variety of contexts, and the standards in ninth and tenth grades expect students to "organize complex ideas, concepts, and information to make important connections and distinctions." In essence, as students develop skills across grades, the Common Core State Standards expect that their writing should appear more and more like an expert discussing a topic.

With that vision of "being an expert" in mind, our students' note-taking can become more purposeful and useful, not just a thing to do because it was assigned. We can teach them to not just gather random notes, but to return to their notes to develop larger concepts, to apply those concepts when moving to new sources, and writing about their research.

DEVELOPING HOW
Students Take Notes

Whether they are taking notes from sources they have gathered or just jumping onto the Internet to gather some quick information, help your researchers learn to take notes in a way that continually pushes them to learn about their topic, not just copy down words.

No matter what strategies you teach, remember that *how* they take notes is not as important as teaching them *why* they are taking them. We can go wrong when we make any style of "notes" have a capital "N," holding students to following graphic organizers to the letter of the law, demanding they complete T-charts a certain way, or always following a particular process. No organizer is perfect for every brain that attempts to use it, so be certain that you hold your students to the habits of thoughtful thinking *more* than checking that they have the right number of columns or absolutely correct steps of a strategy. At the forefront of your students' minds should always be: we are taking notes that help us become experts.

When deciding how you will teach note-taking to your class while also differentiating for individual students, consider a few important things. First, make sure they can read and comprehend the texts they have in their hands. This is, for obvious reasons, more important than anything else (see Chapter 2, p. 11). Once appropriate texts *are* in their hands, be vigilant about their comprehension and thinking. Think of notes as serving a variety of purposes, from supporting understanding, to holding onto larger concepts, to being as multipurpose as a Swiss army knife. Also consider how revision (discussed later in this chapter) can play an important role at all levels of development.

Differentiating Instruction for Note-Taking

Teaching for more emergent researchers

Help students first and foremost read nonfiction texts well. Teach them to use their notes to help them visualize information, to hold onto bigger concepts, and to make connections between ideas. Teach them to revise their notes for domain-specific vocabulary, attempting to use the language of experts.

Teach students to record understandings, not just facts; pausing often to reflect and write about their growing understandings. Show them how to look for patterns in their notes and then read new texts with those patterns in mind.

Teach students to match the type of notes they take to their purpose for reading and the organization of the text; making a timeline, diagram, T-chart, or writing summaries. Teach them to revise their notes often, as a way of synthesizing old and new information into larger concepts.

Teaching for more experienced researchers

▶ **Even Kindergarteners Are Taught, "Find the Main Idea":**
Teach Your Students to Rely on Understanding, Not Tricks, to Hold onto Large Concepts

Teach your students to first focus on comprehension; main ideas can only be found when they understand what they have read. One way to do this is to practice visualizing information, then use those mental images to uncover main ideas.

I have been having a conversation recently with teachers and colleagues: How is it that every year, from primary grades up through secondary, we teach students to "find the main idea" and yet every year they can never seem to do it? Yes, sure, that may be an overstatement; I am sure it is not *every* student that can *never* find the biggest idea of a passage. Though when schools analyze testing data and teachers informally assess their students, it seems that "main idea" is an area with the greatest need. Through conversations, watching students attempt this skill, observing teachers teaching, and reflecting on my own instruction, I have come upon a hunch. I think we too often turn "main idea" into a very special, very mysterious skill with its own set of particular strategies and rules: "You must look for words and phrases that repeat and then throw out any sentence that is extraneous and then also look at the subheadings and then turn them into a question that you will try to answer and then do not forget that also . . ." It is as if we expect students to hunt-and-peck for ideas bouncing around the page, just waiting to be found. Instead, and this sounds obvious I know, we need to first teach them to understand what they are reading. Any work at finding the "main" idea naturally must come first from comprehending what you read.

One strategy that can support comprehension of informational texts, as well as finding main ideas, is to visualize. That is, read a few sentences and form a picture in your mind. Continue reading, and when the images you are creating seem to change a lot, then stop. Replay the images you've already made and ask yourself, "Which pictures did I see the most?" For a Science class of fifth graders I might demonstrate using *Looking at Cells* from the *National Geographic Reading Expeditions* series (2003). I could say:

> **"If we are reading to become experts on our topics, it is often really difficult to memorize all of the hundreds of facts contained in any one book. So instead, we can stop every so often to consider a main idea we want to take with us when we finish reading. It is a lot easier to remember seven really big ideas than it is to remember tons and tons of smaller facts. Plus, when you stop to pull out an idea, it helps you remember where in the book that idea came from so it is easier to locate again later.**
>
> **"One really helpful way to pull out big concepts, or main ideas, is to read making mental pictures, then stopping to ask yourself, 'Which pictures did I see the most?' Whenever I read I quickly make pictures in my mind. I'd like you to make images in your mind right along with me. I'm going to read from this source about cells and then listen as I describe the mental images I am creating:**
>
> > *Surrounding every cell is a cell membrane. At first scientists thought this membrane simply held the cell together and kept everything inside from leaking out. Today we know . . . It allows some things, like certain chemicals, to pass into or out of the cell; it keeps others out. (p. 7)*
>
> **"Okay, I'm picturing a cell. It's kind of like a circle and slimy, moving around. In my mind it's kind of green for some reason. Anyway, I see the cell membrane, like the outline of the whole thing keeping all the stuff from leaking out. I also, though, from that last part we read, see some things going in and some going out. My image is of this big blob with sort of strings of things, chemicals, moving in and out all around the circle. Did you picture something like that as well? Each of our pictures might be a little bit different, and that's okay as long as we try to picture just what the words say.**

"I'm going to read a bit more and then I'd like you to tell someone near you what you are picturing. Let's see if the picture stays close to the same in the next part or if it changes a lot:

> *The cell membrane is very choosy. It has places that work like little doors. If the right kind of chemical comes along, the "door" will open and let the chemical in or out. (p. 8)*

"Okay, tell your partner what you saw and if the image stayed close to the same or changed . . .

"It sounded like the images stayed the same. Remember, we will keep reading until the image changes. When it does, we'll stop and make an idea. Let's keep reading:

> *Plant cells and one-celled organisms called bacteria have another layer—a cell wall—surrounding their cell membrane . . . (p. 8)*

"I think I need to stop there. The picture in my mind started to change from just a cell with a membrane to now a cell with a wall around it.

"Once we stop we then can replay in our minds all of the pictures we have made so far and ask, 'Which pictures did I see the most?' Could you open up your notebook and quickly jot down one sentence, say what picture you saw the most? What was the main picture, or main idea, you will take with you from what we just read?"

It is amazing how effective this strategy is. Because students are focusing on making visual images, they are focusing a great deal on understanding.

When Naomi, a fourth grader at an elementary school in Farmingdale, New York, was having trouble noticing different ideas within one chapter of a book on spiders she was reading, visualizing helped her better see the invisible breaks within the text, the groupings of information. I said, "Okay Naomi, could you pick up that sticky note where you wrote, 'spiders eat different things' and hold it next to each paragraph in this section? I want you to ask yourself, 'Does the picture I get in my mind from this sticky note match the picture I had in my mind when reading?'"

She started with the first paragraph: "Yep, I saw in this section all of the animals and the bugs they eat. And in this next paragraph," she paused. "Oh! I get it. Oh wait, I see! These two paragraphs on the bottom of the page. I was picturing spiders using venom and sucking out their prey's insides. Oh, it's actually two different ideas." She picked up a new sticky note and wrote a second main idea: "Spiders bite and drink their prey's insides."

The key, again, is helping students really understand what they are reading, not just jumping to attempt to make a main idea. Relying on visualization is just one of hundreds of strategies for supporting nonfiction reading comprehension. You might turn to other professional texts to support them even further, such as *Navigating Nonfiction* from the *Units of Study for Teaching Reading* series (Calkins and Tolan 2010), which provides a unit of study on teaching students to read both expository and narrative nonfiction with agency, and *Strategies That Work* (Harvey and Goudvis 2007), which suggests a whole host of reading and jotting strategies applicable to nonfiction reading.

DEVISING TEACHING THAT MATCHES YOUR STUDENTS

• More Experienced Researchers May Benefit From:

More experienced researchers are not immune from misconceptions around main points of articles. One common issue is that they become so gifted at making broad, expansive inferences that they begin to confuse their thoughts from those of the text. In Education for Thinking (2005), professor Deanna Kuhn points out how serious this issue is for any learning: "If students are not clear whether their claim is based on their existing beliefs or the new information they have examined . . . they are not in control of the process of theory-evidence coordination in their own thinking" (p. 75). You might teach students to fall into the habit of stopping often to mark what in their notes is directly from a book and what are their own ideas. Teach them to literally underline or cite book phrases and ideas, and not do so with their own thoughts and opinions, so later they can see the difference.

• More Emergent Researchers May Benefit From:

More emergent researchers may need to not just jot the "main image" or main idea when using this strategy. It may be a helpful scaffold, to push them to actually stop and picture over and over, if they sketched or jotted what they were picturing. You might teach them to stop every two or three sentences, sketch or jot quickly, read two or three more, sketch. And so on. Then go back and look at what actual pattern they see in all of them.

• Using in Content-Area Classes:

Guiding concepts, the stuff content-area teachers give blood, sweat, and tears for, can actually become quite expected within content-area nonfiction reading. Students will greatly benefit from going into a new source, first stopping to say what they can already expect will be topics or ideas in that text. A book on animals? Of course there might be survival, specialized body parts, the life cycle, and so on. A historical figure? Of course life in the time period, early life, rise to power, and so on. Having these expectations in mind can help students find ideas that feel larger and important to the topic, not smaller details.

• Additional Strategies:

When jotting down main images or ideas, students sometimes begin to ramble on and on, listing every last detail. Teach students one way to get used to describing tighter, more focused ideas is to hold up two hands and put down one finger for each word they say, with a goal of not using much more than six fingers. Show them how they should keep practicing until they get it down to around that few: "Spiders, build, webs, that, match, their, habitat." Often I will have partners do this together. In a sixth-grade class one boy asked, "Is it okay to use five fingers instead of six?" He was very proud of the focus of his idea.

▶ Slow and Steady Wins the Race: Teach Students to Paraphrase Well by Pausing to Think

Teach students to pause to reflect on their reading before jotting notes. One strategy is to read a section, then cover it up and jot notes about their learning, then go back and reread that same section looking for details or technical vocabulary they need.

One critical habit to teach students, one that can live within any format of notes, is to adopt a mental pause. Literally, pause for a moment to think. As adults we do this more automatically; if I am writing and get to the word "tomorrow" I pause for a moment: "Is it two m's or two r's?" If we are reading, writing, cooking, skiing, whatever, and trying to be really good at it, we often pause in the midst of things to mentally check in. This is an important learning habit. The "stopping to think" moment gives you a chance to think bigger, to find those larger patterns or concepts. Literally speaking, it is tough to memorize every word on the page if you are *not* looking at it, so looking up to stop and think forces you into a brief and essential synthesis. We can teach students to do this and then show them that after they pause, they can reread, seeing if there are essential ideas or vocabulary that should be included. I have come to call this "read, cover and jot, reread."

When demonstrating this for a class of eighth-grade students, I used an informational book about sharks, *Sharks* (McMillan and Musick 2008), for my demonstration. I showed them the first few steps by reading a short section on parts of a shark's body:

> **"When we read we have to be certain we are not just looking at words going by on a page; instead we have to remember that we are reading to become experts. To learn all we can about a topic. One way to do this is to force ourselves to pause to think. Watch how I read a bit, then cover it up and pause. I jot down what I learned, then reread to see if there is any key information I forgot to include. First I'll read:**
>
> > *Every moment of a shark's life, its internal organs are working like the parts of a living engine. Sharks have many of the same organs that people do, such as a brain, a stretchy stomach, kidneys, and a blood-pumping heart. But a shark's insides are also adapted to undersea life. The gills move oxygen from seawater into the shark's blood and get rid of the waste carbon dioxide. A liver packed with oil makes a shark more buoyant so that it needs less energy to stay afloat and swim. (p. 12)*

"Now I'm going to cover this page, pause a second to think, and jot down what I learned. I can't remember everything, so I just have to think about what the most important ideas were. Watch what I jot down." I wrote:

> *Shark bodies have some parts similar to humans. Though they also have some organs that have different characteristics than ours, like their liver is filled with oil and it helps them float, and they have gills.*

> **"I'm now going to go back and reread the book. This time, I am going to read looking for ideas, concepts, or even vocabulary that an expert on this topic would know. After reading, I'll go back and add to my notes only those things I think are most important to making me more of an expert. I could add them as new sentences, or maybe I'll just make small notes in the margins and draw lines. The way you add those notes is completely up to you; what matters most is that they help you develop greater expertise on your topic. Watch how I do this . . ."**

I reread, then revised my entry as shown in Figure 3–1.

I often end by pointing out that my notes, because they are my own, do not need to be perfect. I did not have to go back and rewrite this paragraph or erase everything or tear the whole page out. These lines and arrows show how my ideas about this topic are growing and changing. I find that if you celebrate and even encourage more freedom in their note-taking, you will be better suited to see just how their minds are working. The additions are not mistakes; they are indications of the birth of new or revised ideas.

Figure 3–1 A Stop-Cover-and-Jot Revised Entry

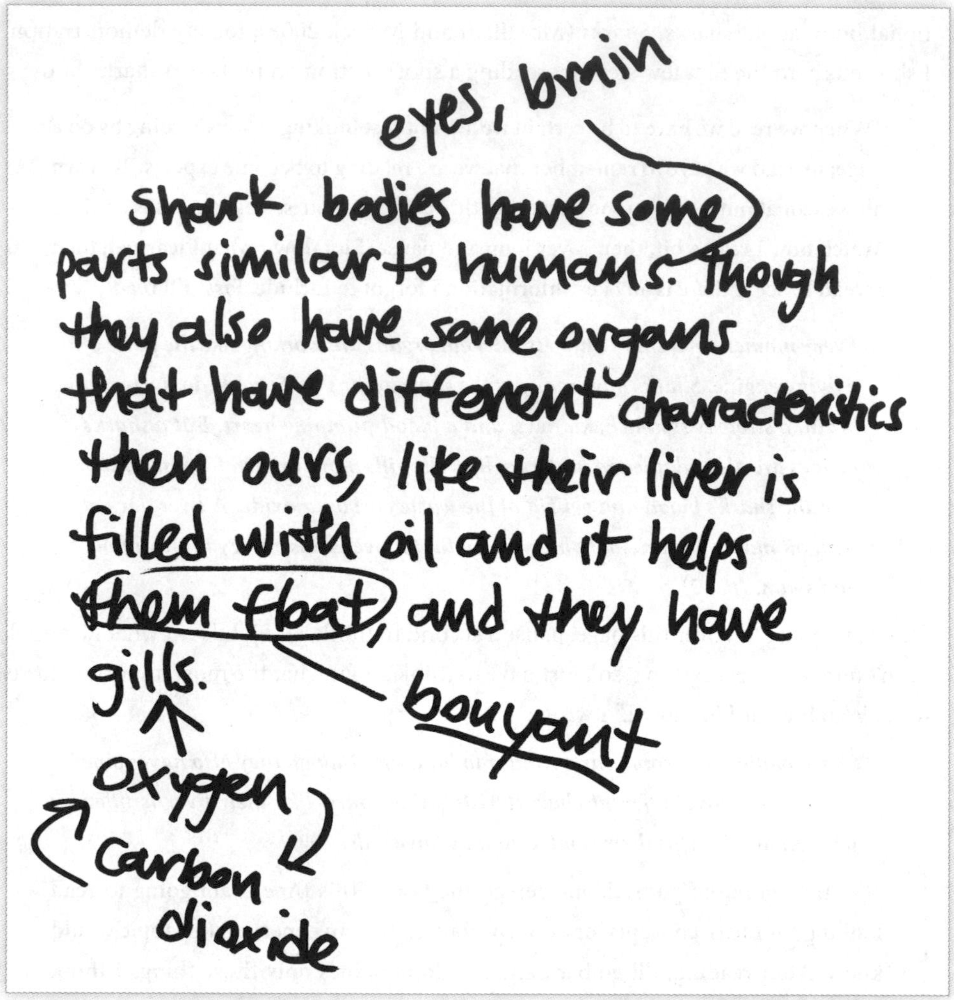

handwritten note:

eyes, brain

Shark bodies have some parts similar to humans. Though they also have some organs that have different characteristics then ours, like their liver is filled with oil and it helps them float, and they have gills.

bouyant

oxygen
carbon dioxide

DEVISING TEACHING THAT MATCHES YOUR STUDENTS

• More Experienced Researchers May Benefit From:

More experienced researchers perhaps can learn to shape their learning summaries even more carefully. You could teach them to first hold in their mind the main idea or ideas of the passage they read (perhaps using the strategy "Even Kindergarteners Are Taught, "Find the Main Idea": Teach Your Students to Rely on Understanding, Not

Tricks, to Hold onto Large Concepts," p. 34), then count out on their fingers or think, "What were the main parts of this?" Teach them, then, to jot their learning almost like a body paragraph to an essay, stating first a main idea, then details. It's worth the effort; research has indicated the ability to summarize as an essential skill for student achievement across all content areas (Allington 2005; Carnegie Report 2007).

• More Emergent Researchers May Benefit From:

You might have more emergent researchers practice this a bit orally, pairing partners with the same readable text. Teach them to decide where they will stop, read a bit, then turn to their partner and compare their quick summaries, co-creating some notes, then going back to reread to find information they may have missed the first time. You will need to teach them to listen for differences in their ideas. For example, when partner A says, "sharks' insides are <u>exactly</u> like humans'" and partner B says, "sharks' guts are <u>sort of</u> like people's <u>and also not</u>," it is not enough to just keep moving on. Instead, they should learn to hear that difference and return to the text to verify. This practice helps to build each individual's own internal pause and check.

• Using in Content-Area Classes:

In content-area classes, students can be greatly supported by having in mind predictable lenses for studying topics. It will aid in both how they understand the content they are reading and how they determine what is worth writing down. A group of middle school Social Studies teachers in Queens, New York, helped devise a list of "themes" that students can be on the lookout for while reading. I thought it was a stellar list, such as: "how environment affects cultures," "how unfairness leads to conflict," and "how competition for resources develops actions." Students, then, do not read for just any concept, but can have these and other lenses in mind while reading, helping them notice information that they really should get down on paper.

• Additional Strategies:

Teach students to change the mode of their note-taking to support synthesis. If they are reading text, show them how they can do this same strategy—only instead, read, cover, and sketch, then reread. Turn ideas into sketches with labels. If they are looking at a graphic or chart, in their notes they should turn this into written words. This was particularly helpful with a seventh grader who was earnestly trying to memorize and quickly write down each line of a psychology textbook. When I asked him to instead record the text in diagrams, he found himself stopping to think and really trying to understand what he read.

▶ **On Your Mark, Get Set, Go:** Teach Students to Make Smart Choices About When to Use Which Type of Notes

Teach students to pay attention to information a text is presenting and choose a form of note-taking that will best organize those ideas. One example is to use timelines when a text presents a sequence of events or dates.

No matter what the hobby, you choose tools to match the task: a hammer for nails, then a crowbar to pry that bent nail out of the wall. Teach your students that the same holds true for the thinking tools, the notes, that you are teaching them to use. A researcher can record in any fashion, but as the information in a text changes, some forms of note-taking can more effectively help you develop expertise than others.

The types of notes are endless, everything from T-charts and timelines, to webs and Venn diagrams. In think-tank groups at Teachers College over recent years we have studied how students view and use notes. What has become important is to not just teach students types of notes, but to teach them to make smart choices about when to use which types. Come high school, college, and certainly career, it is less and less likely that someone will assign these things. No one is standing up in a board meeting to say, "I am about to go over some important sales figures. Could everyone please make a Venn diagram in their notes, and write down how this year's net costs and income are similar and different from last year's?"

With a class of fifth graders, for instance, teach them *when* to use a timeline, not just what it is. A demonstration could sound like:

"I know all of you have used timelines at some point. I want to remind you that things like timelines—or T-charts or any other kind of notes—are not just things that teachers assign, but tools you can choose to use. For example, with a timeline, if I come to a point in a text where the author is indicating a sequence of events, for example if they say, 'Four steps lead to . . .' or they start listing dates across a section or chapter (or several chapters), I need to think, 'Hmm, a timeline would really help me keep this stuff straight in my mind.'

"For example, these pages from a book on the American Revolution talk about many events, starting with the Boston Tea Party. When I look at the page there are dates everywhere. I could just list them in my notes or write them into paragraphs, but I know that having a visual representation of time passing will be really helpful for me. It will help me both understand and remember what is going on in these pages.

"So, I *noticed* the page has a bunch of dates in order, so *I know* I can make a timeline to help me organize this information. Maybe I'll write it vertically, instead of horizontally, so I can write the notes on the lines, left to right. I will just jot the dates . . . let's see, there is 1773 . . . and 1774 was the Quebec Act . . . and also the set of 'Intolerable Acts' that same year . . .

"Did you see what I did? I didn't just wait for someone to tell me what kind of notes to make. Instead, I looked at the text I was reading and thought, 'Hmm, a timeline would help me organize this list of events better.' This is true for any type of note-taking: match it to what a text is helping you learn.

"But I want to suggest one more thing before you get back to your work. Don't just pay attention to what the text you are reading is inviting you to create. Also imagine how your notes can help you notice connections, concepts, ideas you didn't grasp at first. Make your notes your own. Consider ways of changing, expanding, revising your note-taking.

"For instance, I could look at this timeline and imagine a way that concepts or connections could be added to it. I could make two timelines, one for what is going on in the colonies and one for what is going on in Britain. Or, I could look for cause-and-effect relationships, drawing arrows from one event to another. For example, how the Boston Tea Party led to Britain responding with the 'Intolerable Acts.'"

At this point do not just assign, "Okay, go make timelines." That would be missing the point. Instead, help students remember the kinds of note-taking strategies they know, from your class, from other classes, and even from other grades. Timelines are just one such strategy. You may want to make a chart together, or add to one you have already started, as shown in Figure 3–2.

To test their understanding of this lesson, ask them to briefly skim a page from one of their sources and tell a partner what kind of note-taking would help them organize their thinking about that particular page. Do not assume, of course, that just because you classify a chart by type every student will know how to use it. Instead, think of the chart as something that will give those students the ability to run and run and run with this idea. It will also be a reminder for you of other types of note-taking to teach in future lessons, with groups or with individuals. What matters is deciding when to use types of notes, not just doing the strategy you just taught.

Figure 3–2 "Types of Note-Taking We Already Know" Chart

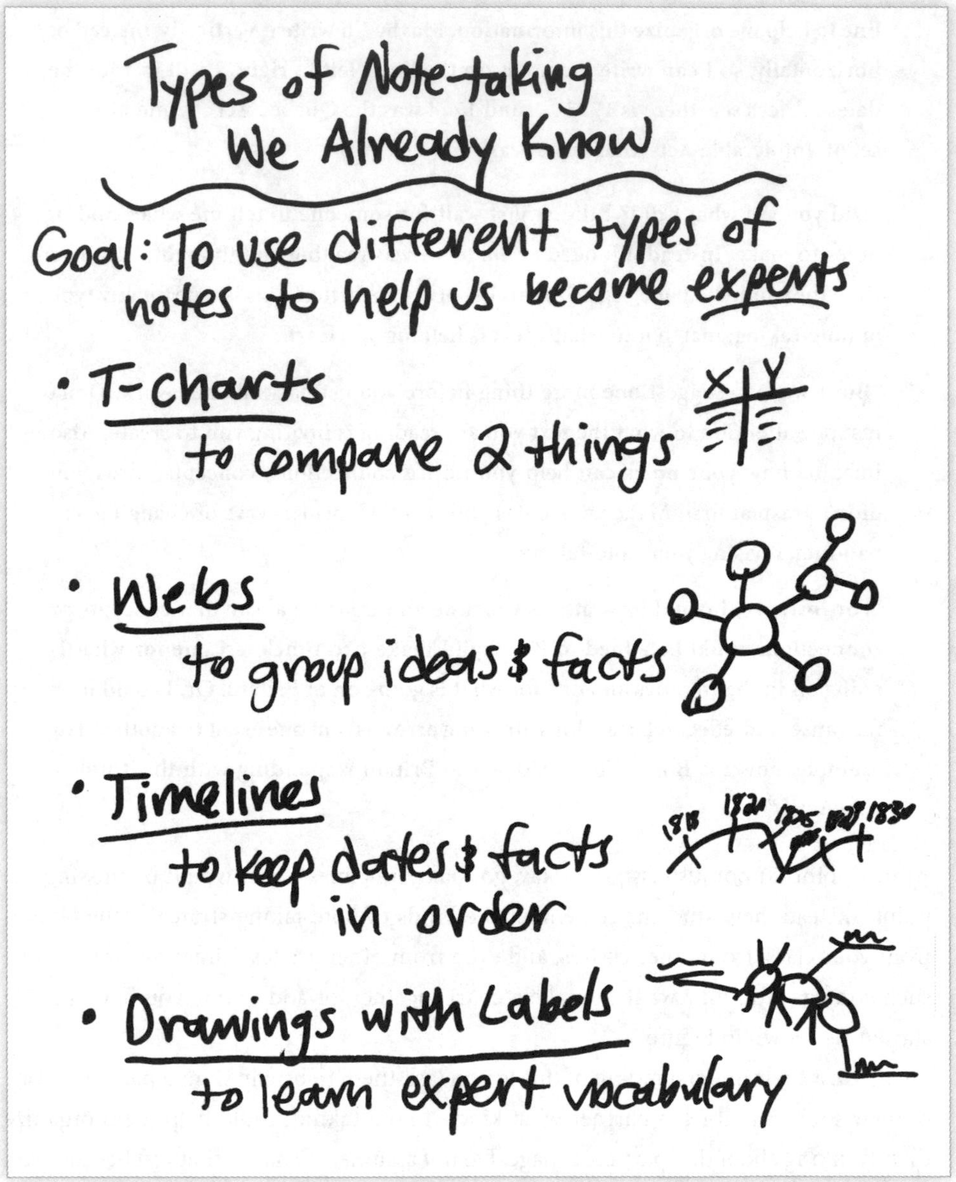

Types of Note-taking We Already Know

Goal: To use different types of notes to help us become expents

- T-charts
  to compare 2 things

- Webs
  to group ideas & facts

- Timelines
  to keep dates & facts in order

- Drawings with Labels
  to learn expert vocabulary

DEVISING TEACHING THAT MATCHES YOUR STUDENTS

• More Experienced Researchers May Benefit From:

More experienced researchers should be encouraged to make variations on any type of notes that best support them in seeing bigger concepts or connections they may have otherwise missed. A way to do this is to combine multiple types, either repeating one (like in the case of a double or triple timeline) or putting kinds together (as in placing a T-chart on a point in a timeline, or making a web of Venn diagrams). Some of this will just be fun experimentation, but you should always connect students back to thinking, "What type of organization is the text pushing me to have?" The usefulness of the notes is more important than just making them.

• More Emergent Researchers May Benefit From:

More emergent researchers might benefit from studying words and phrases authors use to indicate to readers the teaching that will follow and then using them as a good format for their own notes. Help them look especially at opening paragraphs to sections for phrases that indicate a kind of organization, for example, "The two kinds of . . . are very different . . . ," which would indicate that I might want to make a two-column chart or perhaps sketch and label the differences between two things. If the author wrote "The life cycle of a . . . ," then I should know that a timeline or flow-chart would help me remember the cycle in order.

• Using in Content-Area Classes:

In content-area classes, when you feel pressed for time and worried that you can't get to all the examples you want to, allow students to be each other's teachers. One way to do this is to borrow just five or so minutes from a class one day, ask students in groups to study one another's notebooks (flip through a few pages), and on a piece of chart paper, perhaps, list off the most interesting ways students in their group have taken notes. I will sometimes then use the guise of "sharing tips with the class," maybe even on a piece of chart paper, to motivate them to do this well and quickly, but in the end the real learning is from the study of other notebooks.

• Additional Strategies:

Any work that is done with text can often be practiced with video, which for some students makes strategies more concrete and their use more memorable. There is an art to this. If you are practicing matching notes to text or any other strategy with an informational clip, like part of an episode from Animal Planet or PBS, think of your demonstration just as you would with reading or writing. Plan that every few seconds or minutes you will pause to show how you are comprehending the video and how and why you could jot notes. "Hmm, so this documentary on Lincoln just said, 'What he experienced as a child would shape his future.' I am thinking I could get my notes ready. Now, should I use a timeline because it sounds like the documentary will track him over time, or should I make a cause-and-effect chart, like a T-chart? Or both on different pages?"

▶ Scratch That, Reverse It: Teach Students That the Most Important Thing They Can Do for Learning Is to Revise Their Notes

Teach students to continually put together the facts, concepts, and ideas they are generating from various sources. One way to do this is to teach them ways to revise previous notes with new information.

I think we can all agree that revision makes writing better, more interesting, more clearly organized. So why, then, when students are writing about their thinking, do we not have them go back and revise? It is an odd disconnect. While reading texts and writing about that reading, more often than not we have students jotting new, new, new things and rarely teach them to go back to what they have already written and do something with their old notes—to correct misinterpretations, to answer open questions, to revise old thinking with newly synthesized ideas. Now, I did confess earlier in this chapter that I never return to my notes and certainly some people do not. So again, think of this as scaffolding students toward independence. If their note-taking is not currently leading them to more expert thinking, help them return to revise their notes as a concrete, hands-on way to do the abstract work many of us are silently doing in our minds.

For instance, after reading several chapters of one book or after reading other sources on the same topic, return to an original page of notes to revise your old thinking with new. It is actually amazing to consider the journey you have taken since that first page. Think about looking back to a childhood photo of yourself, or you and a friend, or maybe you have kids. Wow. How did we get *here*? Looking back at a "first," especially if you are holding something tangible in your hand, propels you into automatic replay; it helps you put it all together.

One version of this could be to set up spots in their notes as "Return To" pages. Teach your students to leave a few pages open, early in a section or in the back of their notebook or even loose-leaf sheets in a folder, wherever you or they want to put it. After even just a bit of reading, potentially larger concepts will start to arise that could be recorded in these sections, with lots of space left to return to. If I were reading the book *Oh, Rats! The Story of Rats and People* (2006) with a class, I might have jotted across the top of two different pages: "Rats have amazing bodies," "Rats and humans have hurt one another." Or with a different topic, I might have written "Cells are like little machines," or "Segregation came from bigotry and fear," or "Dogs are hard to care for." Leave spaces on these first few pages to return to later on and add to these ideas, revise the facts underneath them, and change the categories altogether as needed. "Hmmm," you think weeks later. "It's not just 'Rats and humans have hurt one another,' it is also that 'Rats and humans have surprisingly helped one another,' too."

Consider Loiza's case, where she organized a few "Return To" pages with big ideas she and her group were finding about ocean life. After reading a few sources she returned to these pages, like the one shown in Figure 3–3, to put a series of facts together.

A different approach—one you could pick up even if you haven't planned ahead—is simply to revise an older page of notes just as you would a draft of writing. Show students how you reread and now add your new understandings between the lines, in the margins, on the back, or even on extra paper. Notes you took early on, when first learning about a topic, can now change with newer information. Doing this is a concrete way of sewing together ideas from across the broad scope of a researcher's reading.

For instance, in a conference with a sixth grader, a teacher and I were showing him how you can revise notes by thinking, "What is this whole text about?" and then going back through your notebook to connect smaller main ideas back to the big one. We were using Jane Goodall's book *The Chimpanzees I Love: Saving Our World and Theirs* (2001) to show him what we meant. We explained that if the central idea is something like, "Goodall feels it's important to protect chimpanzees," then a researcher can revise his notes, trying to connect all the smaller main ideas back to that. We showed him a jotting that said, "This section is about the discovery that chimpanzees make and use tools to eat."

Then we showed him how to have that idea in mind and then say something like, "which connects to the central idea because . . ." and try to finish the sentence. How does using tools to eat connect to the bigger concept in this book—that Jane Goodall feels it's important to protect chimpanzees? Maybe it becomes, "Chimpanzees should be protected because there is so much that people have only recently learned about them" or "Chimpanzees are more like us than people realize. They can use tools just like us, and we should protect them because they can teach us about ourselves."

Figure 3–3 One of Loiza's "Return To" Pages

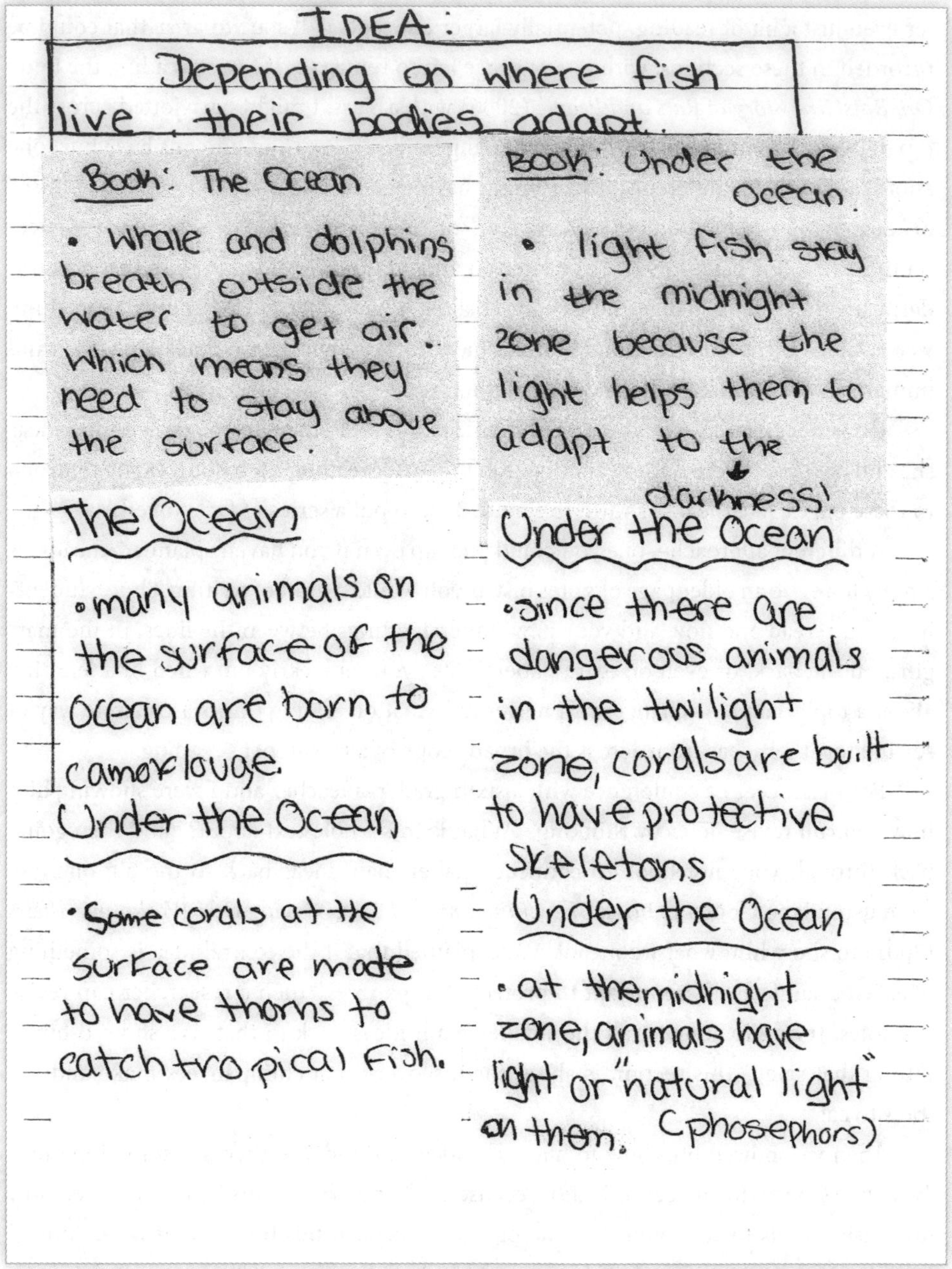

IDEA:
Depending on where fish
live, their bodies adapt.

Book: The Ocean

• Whale and dolphins
breath outside the
water to get air.
Which means they
need to stay above
the surface.

Book: Under the
Ocean.

• light fish stay
in the midnight
zone because the
light helps them to
adapt to the
darkness!

The Ocean

• many animals on
the surface of the
ocean are born to
camorflouge.

Under the Ocean

• Some corals at the
surface are made
to have thorns to
catch tropical fish.

Under the Ocean

• since there are
dangerous animals
in the twilight
zone, corals are built
to have protective
skeletons

Under the Ocean

• at the midnight
zone, animals have
light or "natural light"
on them. (phosephors)

The Common Core State Standards would be ecstatic if students could do this well: to determine central ideas (reading standard 2) and then notice how smaller parts and larger parts of texts relate (reading standard 5).

DEVISING TEACHING THAT MATCHES YOUR STUDENTS

• More Experienced Researchers May Benefit From:

More experienced researchers should be reminded that ideas and concepts are not bound by one chapter or just one book. When reviewing "Return To" pages or going back to old notes to revise them, it is a time to also open up all of their previously read sources (think back to that vision of the student in the Ivy League university, stacks of books around). When they stop to write underneath the concept, "Cells are like little machines," they should not just jot information from this one text but flip back through their notes and other texts to add more. This kind of CCSS reading standards 7 and 9 work—integrating knowledge and ideas from across diverse media and learning and comparing multiple texts—also means that you may need to teach researchers to skim using not just the table of contents (which many are familiar with), but the index as well.

• More Emergent Researchers May Benefit From:

More emergent researchers may need support in determining larger concepts or headings to connect information under. Some texts are decidedly built for this, where a major idea is present, even from the cover, title, or blurb on the back. In which case, as with the Jane Goodall book, teach students to review these. With other texts, though, especially those where the topic is very broad and the title is something like "Spiders" or "World War II," it probably pays off less to consider a major idea for the entire book. Instead, a reader may focus more on bigger ideas inside a chapter or section. A student might read a chapter title and think, "This chapter seems to be mostly about the Boston Tea Party" and then learn to revise this to be even more specific by connecting smaller main ideas back to this larger idea. For instance, revising their idea to be: "The Boston Tea Party was caused by people feeling mistreated."

• Using in Content-Area Classes:

In content-area classes you may sometimes choose to stack the deck a bit, providing your students with a few larger categories to make as "Return To" pages in their notebooks, especially if you are concerned about particular content standards in your state that you want to be certain they are working toward. In a Science class, for example, you might ask students to set aside a few pages and make a T-chart with "Plant Cells" on one side and "Animal Cells" on the other, if the main purpose of that unit of study is comparing and contrasting these two kinds. Then show students that when you revise you do not just list everything there is to know about those topics; instead you still put larger concepts underneath each: "cell structures" and "how cells reproduce."

DEVELOPING HOW
Students Gather Domain-Specific Vocabulary

Words are amazing tools. They allow me to transfer the ideas I am holding in my head to your mind simply because you are reading a bunch of characters that make up words that stand for ideas. If I use my words really well, and choose them carefully, I could actually implant my thoughts in your head, perhaps even if at first you disagreed with them. If we get into a conversation, our sharing of words back and forth can allow us to imagine almost anything together, and if we had the right skills we could turn those words into action.

Experts develop nuance in their language to describe with more and more specificity exactly what they are intending to communicate. A doctor writing notes on a patient to a surgeon doesn't just say "broken bone" but specifies "fracture to left tibia below the patella," so the repair work begins in the leg, not accidentally the arm. The English translator Michael Shuster warns the reader in the translator's note to *The Taste of Wine: The Art and Science of Wine Appreciation* (1996), "A particular problem in this book is that in many cases there is no single equivalent English word for a specific French wine term, especially where there is no context." French wine producers, you see, have refined the words they use down to the minutest degree. A grape in the wrong soil, picked at the wrong time, bottled in the wrong varietal mixture, could cost an entire season's income.

When we have our students work with the terminology of their topics, what the CCSS refer to as "domain-specific" vocabulary, we would be missing a big opportunity if we did not put language into this sort of dramatic context for them. Too often vocabulary work looks like lists of words doled out and students filling in worksheets or looking up words in dictionaries. They are told to "use these words in a sentence," and instead of putting much meaning behind the entire piece, students just slap together sentences in awkward fashion: "She was so loquacious coming into the classroom. The air conditioner in the room made it frigid. Then she read about the protagonist in a book." Ugh. Instead, a study of word usage can be exciting, can feel critical and empowering, because it molds the way we write and talk. It literally changes readers' and listeners' minds.

Differentiating Instruction for Gathering Domain-Specific Vocabulary

Teaching for more emergent researchers

Teach researchers to return to old notes and revise them for more domain-specific vocabulary, replacing general or everyday terms with specifics. Support them in organizing sections of their notes with word banks, glossaries, margin notes, or even just highlighting terms to refer back to when they begin writing.

Show students how to not just revise old notes for more specific words, but then to use those words within any future note-taking, essentially writing and talking as experts. Teach them to focus first on those terms that appear often in texts on a topic, avoiding writing down *every* new word.

Teach students to pay attention to not just new vocabulary, but nuance in words—if there are synonymous words or levels of gradation that arise across sources. It is also important to pay attention to differences between informational word usage and opinion word usage. (Connect this with Chapter 1, "No More Handouts.")

Teaching for more experienced researchers

▶ **Without Lists to Memorize:** Teach Students to Revise Their Notes to Include (and Learn) Domain-Specific Vocabulary

Teach students to return often to notes they have taken and replace general terms with more specific ones. Show them how to return to sources strategically, or use the Internet as a reference book, and revise their language.

An expert sounds like an expert. They do not just have facts in their heads; they also know terminology that is specific and nuanced. As our students learn more about their topics, it is important that they write and speak in that language. One approach is to return to old notes in a similar fashion to the strategy described in "Scratch That, Reverse It" (page 46), when students were returning to add in new concepts or clarify understandings.

Teach students to first review their notes to question which terms feel too general, too novice to them. Then teach them to use references to review the words they chose. What feels essential here is that students learn to decide which words to write like an expert, instead of simply trying to rewrite all words.

When teaching this to a class of fourth graders, for example, it can sound like:

"Researchers, I know we are all working to know so much about our topics that we could teach others. As I look around the classroom, I am amazed to see scientists, historians, etymologists, archeologists, a whole host of experts full of expert knowledge. One thing I would like to point out to you is that experts do not only know a lot, they also write and talk like experts. Meaning, they use words that others in their field would know. Like how when you go to the doctor you sometimes hear him saying very big words to your mom: 'She seems to have a *viral infection*, I think it may simply be rhinovirus, but pay attention that it doesn't become a *secondary bacterial infection*, like *bronchitis*.' The doctor uses these big words because he wants to be very specific; he uses special words about diseases that he knows your mom will know too, so she can get the right medicine or take proper care of you. If the doctor just said, 'She's sick,' your mom would have to guess a whole lot! She wouldn't be sure exactly how to help you. Doctors talk like that because they are experts; they know a whole lot about medicine and illnesses and they use words carefully because they want to be specific. And you know what, researchers? I want you to be able to talk just like that about your topic, just as if you were a doctor talking about health! I want you to know the most important words of the topic you are studying and to write using them and talk using them.

"We can use expert language even right now, as we are note-taking. One way to do this is to look over our notes and circle any words we think are *everyday* language, words we might already know or we think we can find better words for. Here are two jottings I have recorded while reading. I want you to watch how I look for words on one, then I'm going to ask you to help me with the other. I will read and circle words that I think could be more expert. I wrote:

Volcanoes are big mountains that hot red liquid comes out of. The red-hot liquid can burst out of the top and go down the sides.

"Okay, so let me see, which words do I already know could sound more expert or which ones do I think I could find better words for? Well, I think I should circle "hot red liquid" and "go down the sides." When it comes out, I remember it's called "lava," I just didn't write that down. So I can change that right away. I also think there was a special name for when it was inside the volcano, but I forget, so I'll have to look that up. And I'll also circle "burst out of the top"; I think the expert word for that is "erupting.""

I often will then show students a second jotting and ask them, alone or with a partner, to choose the words that could be more expert.

DEVISING TEACHING THAT MATCHES YOUR STUDENTS

• More Experienced Researchers May Benefit From:

More experienced researchers will benefit from not only studying their own notes for words, but noticing when in a text or across several texts a term is used repeatedly. They might think, "Well, if other experts write using this word so much, then I should, too." Teach them to be aware of the "I've seen this somewhere before" feeling.

• More Emergent Researchers May Benefit From:

More emergent researchers might find it supportive to create glossary sections in their notebook or jot in the margins of pages. Glossaries seem to be especially useful when definitions are not copied from books or dictionaries, but instead examples are jotted down from students' understanding of their sources. Additionally, having students write "not examples," or descriptions of what the word is not, can help them have a more specific understanding of new terminology. They might make an entry, "incisors" for example, and write "are teeth" but "are not all teeth, just the pointy big ones in the front." As in the demonstration above, it is important to not teach (or allow) students to make every single word a glossary entry.

• Using in Content-Area Classes:

Content-area terminology sometimes feels like it is the content. If you don't know "allied forces," then you miss a huge part of understanding World War II. Engaging thoughtfully with revising understandings and vocabulary often is a huge piece of the game. In addition, consider the importance of conversation. You might decide to hold some class conversations to synthesize current understandings. When students are talking, you can jump in and say, "Is there a more specific term for that? Can everyone try to use it from now on in this conversation?" Or even go a bit farther and teach a term: "Actually a good word for that is 'treaty.' Can everyone make an effort to use 'treaty' while we talk and later when you write? I'm going to write it here on this chart."

• Additional Strategies:

My colleague Kristi Mraz often talks with students about vocabulary words being objects. Essentially, she says, they're just like the things you love—like dinosaur models when you are young or video games when you are older. You can gather words, too, treating them just as you would beloved objects: collecting them all in one place, comparing them with one another, talking about them and trading them with friends. Thinking in this way can lead to so many creative possibilities for your classroom. In a third-grade class, for instance, the teacher made a tree on her wall where students would collect "leaves" of new words they discovered out in the world; they called these "wow" words. Whenever students were talking they could say to one another "use a wow word," and it was remarkable how quickly students would revise their talk to be more specific or more academic. It seems like an obvious leap to using collected and traded "wow" words within research notes at any grade level.

▶ You Say Tomato, I Say Heirloom Jubilee Tomato Cultivar: Teach Students to Notice Variation and Gradation in Domain-Specific Vocabulary

As students read across texts, teach them to pay attention to the variety of terms used to describe similar ideas or concepts. It is important to notice if these terms are synonyms, if they describe a gradation of an idea, or if they are attempting to show bias or a point of view.

We have all seen students attempt to use a thesaurus with unsuccessful (though extremely endearing) results, describing someone as being "enraged" when all they really meant was "bothered," because they looked up the word "angry" and just picked randomly. Understanding the gradations of words, or even more basically knowing if words carry equal meanings or not, is important to research reading and writing.

One way to teach students to do this is to learn to pay attention, as they learn from sources, to how ideas and concepts are described across these sources—maybe to keep a word list or add to glossaries when terms diverge from what one has been used to. The first step, really, is just awareness.

Once those variations of terms are collected, then you could take the long way—perhaps more thoughtful and sophisticated, but nonetheless long—and reread texts that the different permutations of terms came from to attempt to study their meanings. Or take the quicker route and just look them up. Any good word processor has a "dictionary" function, and the Internet has hundreds more. Good search engines let you type in "What does _____ mean?" or "Define _____" or even "What is the difference between _____ and _____?" and the answer will often pop right up.

In regards to vocabulary instruction, author and researcher Ken Pransky suggests that classroom vocabulary "word walls" are best organized by meaning, not simply alphabetically. That when words are organized to show relationships they are more easily learned (Oct. 20, 2010). Students, when collecting their own domain-specific vocabulary lists, can apply this same thinking. They can revise or reorganize lists to show the relationship of terms to one another. If words, for example, mean the same thing, place them together. If there is a hierarchy, place them in that high-to-low or big-to-small system. Make diagrams with labeled parts or write clear definitions.

For example, when Sally was studying wolves she came across a variety of terms to describe them. She made the chart shown in Figure 3–4 to show the relationship of terms to each other.

Figure 3–4 Sally's Wolves Terminology Entry

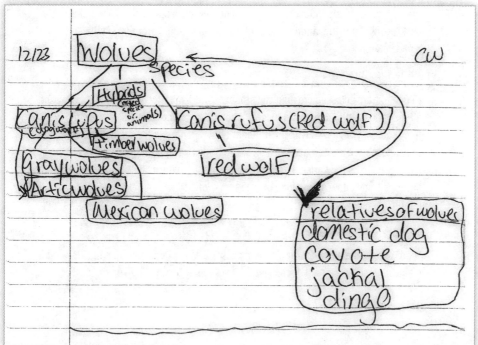

She organized her notes with two main species names and the names of wolves that fit underneath those. As she was writing she realized that "hybrids" and other related names did not fit underneath species names. She listed animals related to wolves on the side with arrows to show they were similar though not exactly the same.

DEVISING TEACHING THAT MATCHES YOUR STUDENTS

• More Experienced Researchers May Benefit From:

More experienced researchers could be taught to create new notes, a new system of organization, to record these nuances—for example, continuums (like timelines) that show gradations from least to most (as in the bothered-angry-enraged scenario) or most specific to most general, or whatever other way the terms are used.

• More Emergent Researchers May Benefit From:

More emergent researchers may be more likely to notice variations in terminology that appear within diagrams. So you might begin this study by first looking at a variety of diagrams from across texts, like a bunch of pages showing labeled wasp bodies, noting that some go into deeper levels of detail than others and it helps to have all of those diagrams open at the same time (or charts or even photographs with different captions) to notice what new information and terms can be derived from them. One graphic labels a part "midsection," while another more specifically labels that same part "thorax," and still another calls it three parts in one: "prothorax," "mesothorax," and "metathorax."

• Using in Content-Area Classes:

In content-area classes creating classroom "word banks" can help students pay more attention to terminology and notice variations. This could be a chart up on the wall that together you add to with any random term. Or you might make charts for larger topics that students can, using sticky notes or just writing on the chart itself, add new terms to as they arise. For example, you could make a chart titled "human body systems," and allow students to post terms, group them, and rearrange them over the course of a study.

• Additional Strategies:

Word choice is also a tool for affecting people's perceptions and opinions. You might teach students to first ask themselves, "Does this source/section seem to have a clear opinion, or are they attempting to provide information as balanced as possible?" If the text does seem to take a side of an issue, then teach students to first realize that word choice may be biased on purpose and they should be careful not to take descriptions purely as fact (as in, do not assume that there is a breed of rat called "disgusting rats"). To check on this, teach them to look across sources for use of that terminology, checking if most sources use that same jargon or not. If there is not a pattern, be suspicious enough to at least check—it doesn't mean that it is the wrong word to use, it just means it needs to be looked into.

Reflecting on Student Growth

As you support students in developing note-taking strategies, worry less about students doing strategies perfectly. Remember that these should not be notes with a capital "N." Instead, look for notes that suggest a student is developing expertise. As you look again for quantity and quality, see if students are accessing a variety of ways of thinking about their topics and writing about them in a way that does not feel like they are just recopying sections of text but instead are developing larger concepts as well as forming their own ideas about the topic.

Figure 3–5 shows two pages from Brianna's notebook to reflect on.

To assess quantity, notice the variety of strategies she is using and if there are some that could support her further. She appears to be:

■ Considering how terms relate (Coral Reefs is marked as "part of" Marine Varieties)

■ Pausing to think and record her learning, not just sections of text

■ Making some choices about types of notes to take (there are lists, sketches, some question-and-answer notes that she invented, as well as a large reflection section after her notes)

■ Finding larger ideas to hold onto (corals are deadly and "sneaky" even though they look harmless)

Consider if there are strategies she has not used that would help make her note-taking even more effective.

Figure 3–5 Brianna's Notebook Entries

To assess quality, evaluate the helpfulness of her note-taking and in particular reflect on the research on expertise from early in this chapter. Does she have notes that will help her remember some facts, hold onto larger concepts about those facts, and apply concepts across contexts? It appears she has:

- Many facts, that appear accurate (about coral reefs and how coral eat)
- Some concepts (corals being deadly)

Consider if there are opportunities for her to apply concepts across contexts. For example, are there things that are true about coral reefs that also could be true about lion fish? What could you teach her to look for or pay attention to that would help her not just with these two pages of notes but with the future notes she takes?

Your feedback and analysis can support your students in moving away from indifferent, copied notes into recording and reflecting in ways that develop their expertise.

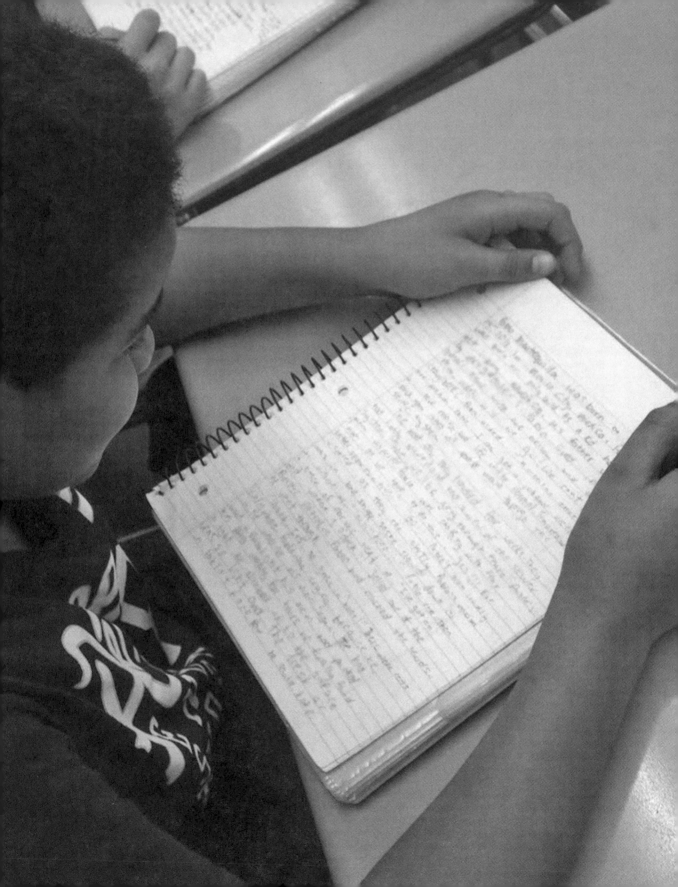

CHAPTER 4

Beyond "Put It into Your Own Words"

Teach Students to Write to Teach Ideas, Not Just Regurgitate Facts

Great nonfiction writers become stars. Within the circle of their readers their names are praised. You probably know people who talk about their favorite columnists as if they were close friends: "That Maureen Dowd, she never holds back." The world has bought millions of copies of books by Carl Sagan and Stephen Hawking. Co-workers trade quotes from *Freakonomics*, *Outliers*, and *The Omnivore's Dilemma*. Some teachers say "Seymour Simon" and "Bobbie Kalman" with quiet reverence as if they are shorthand for, "Of course we all know their books are terrifically written."

What do all of these writers have in common? It is certainly not just that they know a whole lot about their topics; it's doubtful that a book full of dense facts alone would be a number-one best-seller (when's the last time you read a textbook for pleasure?). What great nonfiction writers—best-selling, most-quoted, most highly praised nonfiction writers—have in common is that they do their very best, work their hardest, to be excellent teachers. They work to be engaging, clear, and always with sight of learners in mind. Terrific nonfiction does what all of us educators strive to do every day when we step into a classroom.

Now keep this in mind as you take a little mental journey to the most recent time you worked with your students on research writing. Did your teaching and their writing include this same passion for readers, the same engagement with topics, the same drive? Or did you instead hear yourself saying over and over: "Please, please, just put it into your own words."

As our students move to writing about their research, a good chunk of what has become typical copying from the text will already be pushed aside if they have learned to note-take thoughtfully. There is still the chance, however, that their writing may feel dry, that the great thinking they have done while note-taking will turn to little more than moving their notes from their notebook to draft paper.

When we move research writing away from "proving you read" to what I would like to call "teaching-through-writing," we empower our students to actively craft nonfiction. Shifting research writing from *regurgitating facts* to instead *teaching readers* not only makes their writing better, it continues to help them learn about their topic. One student, Sumayea, summed this feeling up when working on more *teaching* through research writing with her eighth-grade class. "It involves more thinking. You really have to concentrate on it," she said. "When I researched I didn't really think to use my voice and my ideas, I just restated facts. Now I'm thinking more."

DEVELOPING HOW
Students Teach Facts to Others Through Writing

It is a challenge for any of us to go from having an idea straight to writing a great draft; often there is a good deal of mulling over just what to say and how to say it in between. For some writers this is an internal practice in reflection; for others it involves ink to paper or typing words on a screen. It is important that we support our students in a similar process of pondering and practice. Teaching them to experiment with different ways to develop their ideas (described in this chapter) and trying out how they will organize their pieces to best teach their audience (described in the next chapter, "Free from Graphic Organizers: Teach Students to Craft Organizing Structures with Their Readers in Mind"). What they try now, before drafting, can be continued after that draft to further revise and refine their teaching-through-writing. The writing process is not, in fact, as linear as we teach it; instead it is often a series of loops from experimenting, to drafting, to experimenting again, and so on.

Before jumping into the strategies in this chapter, consider what materials your students will need. These writing experiments could go in notebooks, just as their note-taking most likely did. Some teachers find it helpful if students can sort, group, and make new versions, so they supply students with half- or third-sheets of paper, which students keep in folders, or envelopes, or even hold together with large clips or rubber bands. (See Figure 4–1.) There is no one way for every student and every teacher. Consider your

Figure 4–1 Slips for Writing Experiments with Clips or Envelopes

purpose and their developing independence and go from there. What is most important is giving students time for what master writing teacher Donald Graves referred to as "rehearsal" (Murray 1978)—this trying out of ideas, mulling them over, having starts and stops, all ahead of committing to any one way.

If this sounds like a move away from premade graphic organizers, ones that tell students what to write and when, it is. Often those worksheets or overly prescriptive assignments represent us taking over the harder work, so students need only mindlessly fill in information, paying little attention to learning. If you are worried that this is a flashback to the notecard boxes of your high school experience, do not fret; the difference here is an important one. The intent of the notecards was a good one: to help students gather information that they could later sort and categorize. Perhaps that is still useful. You see, though, when students record notes, no matter how well organized, and then attempt to turn those into writing, they often end up with dull paragraphs chock full of quote after quote after quote. When instead they take an intermediary step, and move from note-taking to teaching-through-writing, they are already putting those notes through their own filter. They are practicing learning and practicing writing well. The purpose of sorting these experiments, then, is to later help them take these bits of writing and organize them.

When planning your instruction, you will be supporting students in what the Common Core State Standards refer to as "developing a topic" (W.2b), learning to independently draw on a range of techniques that published authors rely on to engage and inform readers. Help them study nonfiction texts to learn a variety of ways to create their writing and to look for missing information.

Differentiating Instruction for Teaching-Through-Writing

Teaching for more emergent researchers			Teaching for more experienced researchers
Give students time to study published nonfiction texts for craft ideas. Additionally, draw clear connections from what they found to be important while researching and what they should highlight as important for readers. Remind them that they know a great deal about their topics and can write from expertise, not just copy from sources.	Help students experiment with a variety of ways of teaching information they have researched. Suggest that they repeat some facts in a variety of different ways, seeing which teaching-through-writing strategies seem the best. Also help them keep track of missing or uncertain information they can search for later.	Teach your researchers to not just use strategies you have taught, but to study published nonfiction they admire and experiment with ways of writing about their research. Show them that the process of writing and reading research is cyclical, that their writing will guide what they research and their reading will shape the scope of their piece.	

▶ When I Grow Up I Want to Be Just Like You: Teach Students to Study Published Texts and Borrow (or Steal) Effective Writing Techniques

Teach students to study published research and informational books, articles, and even other media. One way to do this is to have a class inquiry, holding a brief, guided analysis with a variety of texts.

When learning to write like an expert there is no greater teacher than published books and articles; they can prop us up when we feel stumped for ideas and stand in as engaging and confident models when we wish to inspire our student researchers. They become much-needed extra hands in our classroom. As Katie Wood Ray points out, "I can't help students to write well by myself. I need lots of help doing this teaching work, and I have found that help on the shelves of my library" (1999, p. 9).

If you have supported your students in first gathering sources and writing about them, then they have already done some of the tough work of finding model texts for you. You will probably still want to round out your examples by gathering a few more texts. When looking, treat the idea of "research" as broadly as possible, bringing in samples of any text where the writer had to first learn something and then report on it—articles from professional journals, newspapers, student magazines, best-selling nonfiction books, popular websites and blogs, anything that is engaging, well written, and full of interesting features.

The Common Core State Standards ask that our students can read texts like writers. The second strand of the reading standards, "Craft and Structure," describes readers who do not just read to understand texts and learn from them, but can analyze word choice, structure, and even how "point of view or purpose shapes the content and style of a text" (anchor standards). Looking carefully at nonfiction texts is probably one of the most important ways to do the development work required in writing standards 2a and b, being able to use a variety of writing, formatting, and media techniques (p. 20).

One way to invite students to study published texts with you is to have a brief class inquiry. Grab one text to study as a demonstration for the class and place others around the room, perhaps having students work in pairs or groups as they look at texts they have been reading as well as a few new ones you provide. It helps to create a chart together while working, so you can refer back to it in future lessons and students can reference it at any time. For instance, with a fifth-grade inclusion class, I began the inquiry by saying:

"As we get ready to write about our research, it helps to first study how other authors do this same thing. What is most important to realize is that they do not just write to list a bunch of facts; instead, everything they write is intended to *teach* their information to readers. These writers are teachers. They do things such as pick topics they and their readers will love. They organize their writing in order to teach. And they use a variety of details and ways of teaching-through-writing to help readers really learn.

"I would like us to look back at a bunch of different texts and analyze them, really study what those writers have done, so we can learn from them and try some of this ourselves. I asked you to get out one of your favorite texts from your research and I passed a few around as well. Let's see if we can fill in this chart together with things we are noticing. First, let's look at the cover and table of contents of our books and headings in articles, to see what kinds of topics writers have written about. Look for not just the big topic, but what part or parts of that topic they chose to write about. If I briefly study this book, I'm noticing . . ."

I then went through each point in the chart, demonstrated looking at one text, and then asked them to look at a text or two with a partner for just a few moments. As they spoke I moved around and added bits of what they were saying onto the chart. In the end it looked similar to Figure 4–2.

Figure 4–2 "Nonfiction Writers Are Teachers" Chart

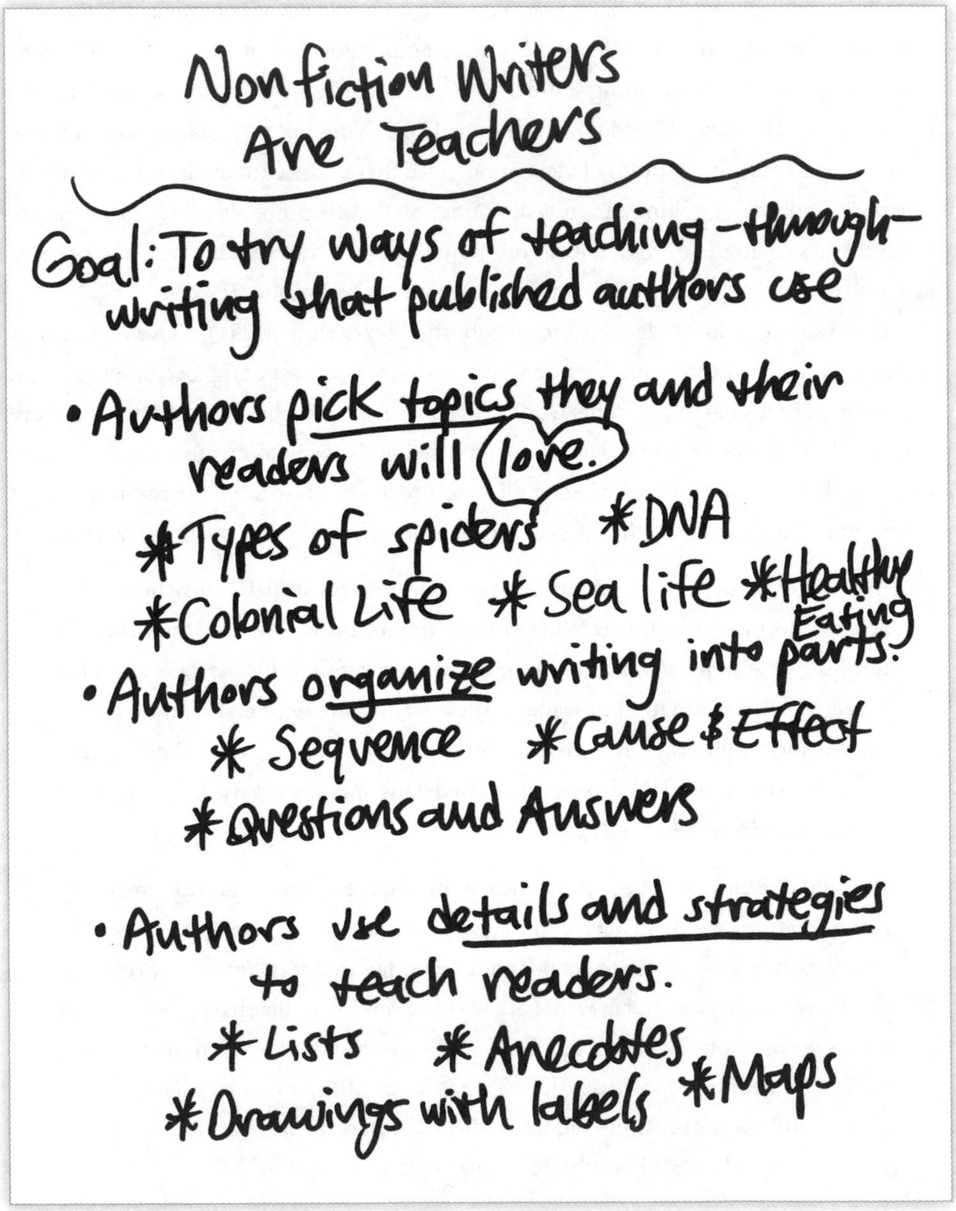

Nonfiction Writers
Are Teachers

Goal: To try ways of teaching -through-
writing that published authors use

- Authors pick <u>topics</u> they and their
  readers will (love.)
  * Types of spiders   * DNA
  * Colonial Life   * Sea life * Healthy Eating
- Authors <u>organize</u> writing into parts.
  * Sequence   * Cause & Effect
  * Questions and Answers

- Authors use details and <u>strategies</u>
  to teach readers.
  * Lists   * Anecdotes   * Maps
  * Drawings with labels

Then, for this first day students were given free range to experiment—jotting lists, making charts, writing bits of text to try out. It felt important to allow them to run with the excitement they built up studying texts. It also provided the teachers and me with a great deal of assessment to run on. We were able to see which areas of research writing students could apply with ease and which needed more careful teaching.

DEVISING TEACHING THAT MATCHES YOUR STUDENTS

• More Experienced Researchers May Benefit From:

More experienced researchers will benefit from analyzing different texts that handle similar subject matter, an expectation of CCSS reading standard 9. Teach your researchers to notice how even though two authors may be writing about, say, the solar system, the way each writes about the topics will vary. From the particular focus, to the information they choose, to the voice of the piece. Your students, then, can be sure to try out not just one, but several different ways of writing about their research.

• More Emergent Researchers May Benefit From:

More emergent researchers might find a large annotated example, posted up in the room, very helpful. A sixth-grade special education teacher in New Jersey made a large poster-size version of a few pages from a student magazine the class regularly read. With the help of the class, she put large sticky notes on different text features and labeled them in student language. For example, she marked a text box as, "Fun Facts box for little facts that don't really fit in the big part." Students referred to the chart often when creating their own pieces, like the boy who made an "antler hunting" fun facts box in his article on moose. (It turns out some moose shed their antlers, and "antler hunters" just go searching for fallen sets!)

• Using in Content-Area Classes:

While textbooks can act as models of nonfiction writing, many content-area teachers have branched out to draw on many more books and articles that are more engaging, more readable, provide more varied perspectives, and are often better written and provide more useful information than textbooks alone (Bauman and Duffy 1997; Budiansky 2001; Allington 2002). It is important to keep in mind that students are able to study how authors write if they are holding texts they can decode and understand. You might indicate the approximate difficulty of texts by indicating a range of levels. You could also remind students to pay attention to how useful a text feels to them, something we do as adults all the time.

> **• Additional Strategies:**
>
> Help your students analyze how authors write. Predictably they will focus the most on visuals in texts, so you will need to guide them a bit to really study the words authors use. You might suggest a few categories of teaching language to search for, perhaps on a chart; then students can add to it by supplying examples of words authors use— for example, categories such as "make comparisons," "give an idea and examples," "say more than one side or opinion," "describe something so readers can picture it," and so on. Then demonstrate how you read a page or two and notice if there are any parts that match these points and what language the author has used.

▶ Don't Just Say the Shark Swam, Bring It On and Let It Swim: Teach Students to Include Narrative Elements in Their Research Writing

Teach students to experiment with one form of teaching-through-writing, creating anecdotes. One way to do this is to choose a fact or two, then for that fact create a character, setting, and describe small step-by-step actions.

Anecdotes play a critically important role in nonfiction writing. Journalists learn to craft their story—*New York Times* editor Francis Flaherty named his book on writing nonfiction *The Elements of Story* (2009)—politicians talk of "spinning the story," lawyers decide how to "piece together the narrative" in the courtroom, and all writers of nonfiction study narrative elements because anecdotes help readers connect emotionally and intellectually with ideas. In fact, the Common Core State Standards specifically add a note to the 6–8 content-area standards, expecting that in Science and Social Studies classes, though students are not required to write narratives, "The Standards require that students be able to incorporate narrative elements effectively into arguments and informative/explanatory texts" (p. 65).

Teach students to first jot down the facts they want to teach to readers. This reminder becomes important so they do not spin their tales so far out that they lose sight of what they are intending to teach. Then help them develop a very short story, using what they know about their topic. Just as in writing fictional narratives, help them decide upon a character or subject, a setting or context, and then describe actions in detail.

In Chapter 3, I demonstrated taking notes from *Sharks* (McMillan and Musick 2008) with a seventh-grade class. From this same note-taking I can demonstrate how I experiment with teaching-through-writing:

"I think the fact that sharks have an oil-filled liver that helps them stay buoyant is really interesting. If I want to use an anecdote to tell this I should first try to picture my subject in my mind (in this case sharks), try to imagine the place it is in (swimming in the deep ocean), and then describe actions small step by small step (perhaps I can describe the shark hunting).

"It will help me to remember if I write the facts I am trying to show at the top of the paper: 'oil-filled liver' and 'keeps it buoyant.' So now, just as we are used to when writing narratives, I'll try to weave together different details as I write, pulling a thread that describes the setting, a thread that describes small action by small action, and a thread that, most importantly, includes facts. Maybe I'll start:

A female shark is out hunting,

then weave in some setting:

swimming quickly past coral reefs.

"Now, I don't remember if sharks actually do live where coral reefs are, so instead of just stopping to check, I will just circle 'coral reefs' and keep writing. It will remind me to double-check that later.

"I am going to keep weaving: action, setting, facts, over and over, in different orders:

Suddenly, she spots her prey up above. The light from the sky above the water shines around a school of fish like a giant neon restaurant sign.

"I have to remember to weave in facts. At the top of my page I wrote 'oil-filled liver' and 'keeps it buoyant,' so I should write that soon, before I get to the end.

Quickly gliding along, rising faster and faster toward her prey. Her oil-filled liver makes it easier for her to rise or fall through the water very quickly. The fish begin to swim away, trying to avoid her, their silvery skins glistening. Her liver keeps her buoyant, allowing her to move quickly up or down in the water to chase after them. In a fast snap, she has caught her dinner. She sinks in her teeth and just as quickly swims away.

"I am going to circle 'swims away' because I am not sure if the shark stays in one place to eat, or leaves with the food in her mouth, or if other sharks come. I'll check that later, too."

I will often highlight in any lesson about teaching-through-writing that students should try similar facts in more than one way. It is important to turn the page, or grab a new slip of paper and try the anecdote once more, perhaps writing about the shark fleeing from danger or preparing to sleep or again hunting but told differently. It is in the telling and retelling that students discover what they most intend to say.

Figure 4–3 Sumayea's Two Narrative Experiments

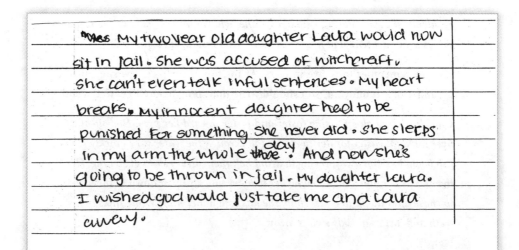

Sumayea tried this strategy when studying the Salem witch trials. She used the same fact, about how even two-year-olds were convicted of witchcraft and went to prison, with two different narratives to see which felt more striking. In her first she described a two-year-old girl wandering around in prison. In her second she tried telling the narrative from the perspective of the girl's mother. (See Figure 4–3.)

Trying more than one way to write about the same facts has left her with two engaging versions to choose from.

DEVISING TEACHING THAT MATCHES YOUR STUDENTS

• More Experienced Researchers May Benefit From:

One concern that is sometimes raised by teachers is that they worry that their students will invent wild tales: "What if they write that penguins can fly? What if they put a car in the middle of an ancient Greek street?" Our more experienced researchers will benefit from learning to skim notes as well as indexes and use the Internet for fast fact-checking. Just keep in mind that if you correct every error for students they will never learn to look for these independently. If you feel really compelled to point out inaccuracies, instead of marking each one, you can just say or write at the top of their writing, "I notice two errors; look again to find them."

• More Emergent Researchers May Benefit From:

More emergent researchers can practice telling small action by small action by experimenting with describing any process or steps they have researched—telling, in detail, how water evaporates and turns to rain, how eagles hunt, or how mountain ranges form. Teach students to use sequence words, varying these based on their sophistication ("first, second . . ." could also be "initially, after which . . ."). Then have them describe minor actions with visual details ("Initially, a puddle of water lies still in the middle of the yard after rain. Next, the sun appears from behind clouds . . .").

• Using in Content-Area Classes:

In her book *Social Studies That Sticks: How to Bring Content and Concepts to Life* (2007), Laurel Schmidt describes a reading comprehension exercise she calls Show Me, "that lets your kids move, gesture, and make faces to show what they understand about a text or story." She says that after reading a passage a teacher might say to the class something like, "Show me what the soldiers were doing during their winter at Valley Forge." This play-acting is equally terrific for writing anecdotes. Students could act out scenes themselves or describe them to peers and ask their peers to "Show"

them, recording what they notice. And this is not just a Social Studies–related strategy. A teacher in North Carolina used arm linking and wiggling to demonstrate what
happens to water molecules as they heat up!

• Additional Strategies:

Another strategy we can borrow from narrative writers is the metaphor. When writers
in any genre compare unfamiliar information to known facts, readers are better able
to understand new concepts. Study these examples in published texts, nonfiction, fiction, and maybe even poetry. Help your writers once again jot down a fact or two they
want to experiment with, then list potential comparisons. Finally, help them borrow
language from other writers, such as "_____ is quite similar to _____, with the main
difference being_____."

▶ Push Beyond Paragraph-Shaped Recopied Notes:
Teach Students to Write from Their New Expertise with Their Notebooks Closed

**Teach students to have a more authentic, expert voice when teaching-
through-writing. One way is to put their notes away and write looking at
key graphics or images to bring to mind all they already know.**

The concept of lifting your eyes up from a text and pausing a moment to consider what
you have learned before taking notes (see Chapter 3, "Slow and Steady Wins the Race:
Teach Students to Paraphrase Well by Pausing to Think") is not only terrific for note-
taking, but is important to carry over into teaching-through-writing.

Another way to support students in synthesizing information, putting all they
have learned together in that moment of pausing, is to teach them to look at visuals—
not text—as they prepare to write, using everything they know as they describe what
they see. This is a great whole-class lesson, but also one well suited for individuals. For
example, I spoke with a boy named Sam as he was putting the final touches on a sixth-
grade Science class project that appeared to be almost totally copied from sources. I
asked him why he did this and his reply was thoughtful and intentional: "When I write
my own words it's too short. So sometimes I have to use parts from books or online so
it's longer." His teacher never said "length" was a requirement, though he perceived that
to be paramount to all else. In his mind, copying was a distant second (or maybe third or
fourth) to filling up pages with words.

To help him remedy his perceived need for copying I taught him to not look at his notes or the recopied pages of a text in his project, but to instead study a visual. Here's what I said:

"So first, I want you to know that your teachers, in fact any teacher you will ever have, will care more about you writing from your own perspective, your own ideas, than just trying to write a lot. So I appreciate your clever thinking that borrowing parts from books will help you write more. But you know what? I think you are selling yourself short. I think you do know a lot about this topic, and can sound very smart about it when you write. I really don't care if you write lots and lots of words, just that you share your thinking.

"One thing I sometimes do, that I want to teach you, is that if I ever feel worried that I don't know enough, or if I just want to try to put a lot of what I have been reading together, I will sometimes look at a visual—a picture or chart or map or something—and then think or talk or write. I know you were writing about child development, but let me first show you an example from a different topic, so afterward you can try this strategy out on your own.

"If I want to try writing about my research on the solar system, but I want to try using my own words, I can turn to a picture or graphic or chart. Like in this book called *Stars and Galaxies*, I can turn to this page that shows a picture of space from the Hubble Space Telescope (*National Geographic Reading Expeditions* 2004, p. 24). I'm going to describe this photo, allowing it to remind me of everything I know. I'm just going to practice it out loud so you can hear what I'm thinking.

"Hmm, well I see many galaxies all over this image, they are different colors and shapes . . . maybe if I were writing I'd say something like: 'Our universe is full of billions of galaxies. Because there are so many, astronomers have classified them into different types.' I am seeing the different shapes in this picture and I remember learning about that. I could add: 'Galaxies have different shapes and there are three main kinds: spirals, ovals, and ones called irregular because they don't have a particular shape.'

"Do you see how I did that? I looked at a visual, not text, to help me put together what I know so far. When I tried to talk about it I realized that I knew a lot more than I first thought. Could you try this with your topic now?"

Sam then did just that, and the transformation was remarkable. What was once a bunch of text that neither he, nor really I, fully understood, became just one paragraph—told from his perspective—of what could become a much longer piece.

DEVISING TEACHING THAT MATCHES YOUR STUDENTS

• More Experienced Researchers May Benefit From:

More experienced researchers may benefit from studying charts and graphs. They may need some demonstration and practice in how to use headings and keys, as well as how these types of visuals add additional information to text. So, if students were writing about planets in the solar system, instead of just writing that Saturn is made up largely of gases, studying a size-comparison table of planets could add to the description. They could now write, "Saturn is almost nine times larger in radius than the earth, but because it is made up almost entirely of gases its mass is only a fraction of our home planet."

• More Emergent Researchers May Benefit From:

More emergent researchers could return to the cover-and-jot note-taking strategy described earlier (see "Slow and Steady Wins the Race: Teach Students to Paraphrase Well by Pausing to Think," page 38 in Chapter 3), only this time use it for writing from their notes. Teach them to reread a page or few of their own notes, then close their notebooks and write trying to teach what they know. Then return to their own notes to check if they missed anything important and revise.

• Using in Content-Area Classes:

In content-area classrooms careful observation is nearly as important as reading text. Teach your students to not just look at visuals, but really to study them as they begin to write. One strategy my colleague at the Reading and Writing Project, Brooke Geller, taught me is to divide any graphic or image into four imaginary quadrants. Then study each one at a time. This simple technique leads everyone, students and adults alike, to look more carefully. After which, students will have even more to say while writing, as they are reminded of other facts the details of an image bring to mind.

• Additional Strategies:

When teaching-through-writing without looking back at notes, it can be hugely in-structive to help students study documentaries and other informational programming, such as PBS NOVA episodes or Animal Planet clips. Invite students to listen carefully to the TV "teaching voice" and practice adopting it themselves, even talking a bit about their topic out loud with partners. While it will not only get a ton of laughs out of your students, it very quickly changes the level of their writing because they start to make more of an effort to "sound" instructive.

▶ **An Ounce of Prevention:** Teach Students to Look for Missing Information While Writing, Not Just After Drafting

Teach students to keep track of questions they need to answer and holes they still have in their information. One strategy is to teach them to reread their writing looking for specific types of predictable misinformation.

Part of teaching-through-writing is knowing what you don't know. We do that as teachers all the time. We think, "How *do* you help students take better notes?" and then we look for books and articles, search the Internet, and ask colleagues. We generally plan ahead for this before lessons; yet there are times when we only uncover confusion afterward. What makes us all better teachers is being aware of these points of needed information and then doing something about it. Our students should learn to be just as mindful about their research writing.

Teach your students to keep notes on needed information while they are writing, to mark spots and jot reminders of information they aren't sure about or realize is missing. In the strategy "Don't Just Say the Shark Swam, Bring It On and Let It Swim" (p. 68) earlier in this chapter, I paused in a demonstration to circle a fact that I wasn't so sure about. It took just a second and then kept me writing. Circling, underlining, starring, whatever coding system your students develop, be sure to show them that as you write you keep asking, "Am I really sure about this or do I need to check?"

Equally, teach your students to reread writing they have already tried out and ask some questions about it. Teachers in Aqaba, a city in the south of Jordan, raised an issue during some of our work together. They said that many of their students—all of whom are English Language Learners—often jump on the Internet to search for information they are missing, but then end up simply copying whole pages of text that they often do not understand. To remedy this, we realized that we had to first teach them to determine what *specific* information they were looking for. The issue is not that students don't know how to search; it is that they often do not first decide what to search for. To help them along, we developed the chart shown in Figure 4–4.

To teach students to do this, I used the chart and modeled my own example, being sure it was full of holes and uncertainty:

There are great places to visit in the seaside city of Aqaba. For example there are some museums. One museum called the Aqaba Museum has a lot to see.

Figure 4–4 "Find Missing Information with Fast Searches" Chart

---

Find Missing Information with Fast Searches

Goal: To make your Internet and book searches faster by searching for specific information

- First, reread your writing to see what information is missing:
  - Do I need to find specific **numbers**?
  - Do I need to find specific **names**?
  - Do I need to find specific **details**?
- Then, search for that specific information:

  - Can I find it in my **notes**?
  - Can I find it in my book **indexes**?
  - Can I find it with a quick online **search**?

I demonstrated how I asked questions from the chart and then marked the text with information I needed to locate, circling "some," the name of the museum I was uncertain of, and "has a lot to see" because I realized I should find out specific sites there.

DEVISING TEACHING THAT MATCHES YOUR STUDENTS

• More Experienced Researchers May Benefit From:

More experienced researchers can be taught to have sources at the ready, moving in a cycle from writing, to reading, to writing again. Additionally, help them see that as holes and questions arise a writer needs to decide if the answer is worth pursuing, or if they should instead refine their topic. For instance, if a student was studying plate tectonics and realized he was missing information on some mountain formations but had a lot on volcanoes, he might decide to refocus his writing and write only about plate tectonics and volcanoes.

• More Emergent Researchers May Benefit From:

More emergent researchers will benefit from keeping their target audience in mind (see "I Feel Like We Have Met Somewhere Before" on page 19 of Chapter 2). Often at our Summer Institute on the Teaching of Writing at Teachers College, we will teach that writers need to approach their writing as if they are strangers. The same holds true for searching for holes in research writing. Often I will have students take on a role, pretending they are someone that really doesn't understand (using a voice like that of the character Steve Urkel from the 90s comedy Family Matters). Having them dramatically overemphasize, "What does that mean?" "What does that even look like?" "Well, how many are there?" is not only funny to watch, but really leads them to question themselves. The voice echoes in their minds even when they are writing silently.

• Using in Content-Area Classes:

In a content-area study teach students to not just mark information that is missing or nonspecific, but also to mark information they have already written down and should fact-check. Teach them predictable points to double-check, like spellings of names, dates of events, and types of measurements (such as inches instead of centimeters).

• Additional Strategies:

After students have learned to mark up texts, you should show them how you ask people, skim books, or search the Internet with specific questions or facts to check. The beauty of the Internet is that everything is there; we just need to find it. The best test subject for this is you. Take some of your students' fact-checking questions and pay attention to how you look for it online or in books. What do you type and retype? When do you skip a link and when do you go ahead and click it? For instance, you might realize that it's important to teach your students that if an index or search engine cannot find the answer to their specific question, ask, "Is there a larger category I should look for or another way to say this same thing?" Or you might realize how adding quotation marks around a phrase tells the search engine to look for that entire phrase, not just individual words.

DEVELOPING HOW
Students Teach Through Text Features

I have to be honest: I think I did not do such a great job starting a unit on nonfiction reading each year. For lack of knowing exactly what to teach, I often would do the age-old default version, the one that goes something like: "Nonfiction has many different features. Let's look. What features are there? Hmm. Oh look, this is called a picture. And under it, look, a caption! These bold words are called subheadings . . ." And so on. It is not to say that our students do not need to be aware of text features; it's just that as they grow older they certainly are ready for more.

I think what I was missing in a lesson like this was that as our students progress through grade levels they need to analyze not just what features *are*, but *how* they are used and *why*—to study the craft choices authors and publishers make to choose one photo over another, to include a particular chart, to bold new vocabulary or not. The good news is that when writing about their research, students can experience this deeper analysis and practice applying it.

When deciding on which strategies to teach, consider the range of types of text features students will study and to what degree they will create their own or search for ones that exist. Most of all, support them in matching these to the main points they are making within their writing—seeing text features as another piece of their teaching readers.

Differentiating Instruction for Teaching with Text Features

Help students study how the texts they have been reading use visuals and teach new vocabulary. Support them in experimenting with these same structures, such as formatting new vocabulary in bold and then supplying text boxes or a glossary.	Demonstrate the thoughtfulness nonfiction publishers and authors use when deciding upon which media to include and how to define new terms. Teach researchers to first consider the main ideas in their writing and then select strategies that best teach those ideas.	Teach students to draw on a variety of strategies. Expect that they will both gather visuals and create their own, applying strategies they have learned in other content areas, such as graph creating in Math. Help them keep their readers in mind, crafting text features to support understanding.	**Teaching for more experienced researchers**

Teaching for more emergent researchers

▶ A Picture *and* a Thousand Words: Teach Students to Carefully Select Visuals to Support Their Text

Teach students to include visuals or other media to support their writing. One way is to demonstrate gathering a variety of images, then selecting the one that most closely matches a writer's central idea.

In the Common Core "Speaking and Listening" set, standards 2 and 5 make a subtle but important leap into embracing media and technology—not going as far as rival standards sets, like the Partnership for 21st Century Skills, but nonetheless believing that students need to learn to comprehend and create information presented in diverse media (Calkins, Ehrenworth, and Lehman 2012). The language of these standards is fairly broad, like in fifth grade when standard 5 reads: "Include multimedia components (e.g., graphics, sound) and visual displays in presentations when appropriate to enhance the development of main ideas or themes." So, um, when is it appropriate? What is a presentation exactly? Though a bit ambiguous, the suggestion to help our students interact, analyze, and be creators of our ever-expanding visual culture can be invigorating.

If you are just tip-toeing into including "multimedia," there is no better type of writing to start with than research. Well-written informational books and videos are chock full of visual elements to help readers learn new content. A simple place to start is teaching students to carefully choose images to add to their writing, understanding that carefully chosen pictures and graphics add to clear teaching. In a workshop at Teachers College, educator and author Pauline Gibbons described a way she helps students engage more purposefully with images in nonfiction while reading. Her explanation has stuck with me and I refer to it often when teaching students to consider images for their own writing (Nov. 24, 2009).

She said that she will often ask students where they think the photos in nonfiction books come from. She will then explain that some people actually have the career of taking particular photos of particular things. For example, they might have the assignment to go to a rain forest and photograph different kinds of frogs in a variety of actions and settings: jumping through the air, jumping from branches, jumping into the water, eating, sleeping, blinking; green frogs, red ones, spotted ones. The photographers' work doesn't stop there, though. They have to take hundreds of photos, then with a book's author sit down and decide what exact photo will best match a certain page of text. They carefully choose between many photos of almost the same thing—all of those frog-jumping pictures—to pick the exact one that will best teach with a page of text about how frogs get around. She will often end by asking how many students would like that job for a living. (I have to admit I was sitting in the audience nodding my head, too. I would love that job.)

Pauline was talking about teaching students to read all the parts of a nonfiction page, but the takeaway for me is that we need to inspire our students to think as writers of those pages, choosing images with care, not just going online, typing "frogs," and cut-and-pasting any image.

When teaching this strategy I often put up a page of text, and it's helpful if I have an Internet connection in the classroom and a projector for my laptop. If not, holding up published books—or even images I printed ahead of time from the Internet—are all worthy fill-ins. For seventh graders I might tell a story similar to Pauline's and then say:

> **"When deciding upon images for our book, we can be just as thoughtful as those photographers. Instead of slapping any picture in, we can first consider what the section we are writing is about, then look over several—even five, or ten, or more—images, then choose the one that most fits the central idea of the section. Lastly, we need to be sure to cite the website it came from.**
>
> **"For instance, here are some sheets I was experimenting with to teach about the lead-up to the Boston Tea Party. If I go online and search for 'Boston Tea Party,' a lot of images come up . . . some are famous paintings, with images of faraway boats in the harbor; some are up close of angry-looking colonists. Here is a pamphlet that was handed out to call people to act, here is a picture of some school**

students today on what looks like a visit to Boston Harbor, and here are pictures of tea and glasses full of tea.

"Wow, that's a lot of stuff. So first I need to go back to my writing and decide what images most add to what I am trying to teach . . . Well, if I read this again, I notice I am really trying to make the point that colonists felt really angry, that this was not just an everyday sort of thing to do, but people really standing up and doing something dramatic to say, 'Hey, look, we're not happy here, pay attention to what we want.' So with that in mind, I can look back at these images and ask, which ones most show or add to that idea?"

In the demonstration I may whittle down the images to two or three, then ask partners to discuss together which ones most closely match the text I was experimenting with. Lastly, I will demonstrate for students how I click-through to find the website address so I can give that site credit for the image. (Chapter 6, "Without Agonizing Memorization: Teach Students to Cite Sources on Their Own," discusses more about teaching students to add citations to writing, including using the Common Core as a guide for how much information is developmentally necessary for different grade-level students to be held accountable for.)

DEVISING TEACHING THAT MATCHES YOUR STUDENTS

• More Experienced Researchers May Benefit From:

More experienced researchers not only can learn to search for existing images, they should be taught to create their own. This can involve some cross-curricular work, creating bar graphs or charts like ones they have studied in Math and Science, or maps like those they have learned to create in Social Studies. Remind your students to keep their readers in mind. If they are creating a bar graph for a group of scientists, then they should probably use plenty of technical language and measurements. If they are creating a graph for readers less familiar with their topic, then they need to be sure that the graphic makes relationships between points of information clear, without being overly complex.

• More Emergent Researchers May Benefit From:

More emergent researchers will benefit from stepping back and setting a teaching goal for the images they find. Teach them to first think of the main idea from their own writing that they are trying to convey, then of their audience and what those readers will need help understanding, and finally some quick jotting about what images they hope to find. With these in hand their image search will be more productive and purposeful.

• **Using in Content-Area Classes:**

In a content-area study students can be taught to look back over the notes they took in response to different sections of text (described in "On Your Mark, Get Set, Go: Teach Students to Make Smart Choices About When to Use Which Type of Notes" in Chapter 3, p. 42), and now apply that same thinking to their own teaching-through-writing. Help them see that if they now want to teach others about key dates, that timeline they created in their notes while reading about the reproduction of a cell could now serve as an excellent graphic. Those cause-and-effect charts they jotted while studying ancient China could fit in nicely as text boxes on the page.

• **Additional Strategies:**

You may teach students to go beyond print images, applying a similar strategy to other "diverse media," as referenced in the Common Core State Standards. Students can be taught to look for video clips or audio, just as they might search for images, finding several options and then choosing the best to represent their central ideas. In the case of longer clips, students can learn to not just find a video, but the brief point in the video that will best illustrate their point. Searching "revolutionary war," for example, on YouTube brings up many video clips. They might choose one from a documentary and then watch to find the portion of the video that connects to their section on "weapons," perhaps a thirty-second clip of men loading muskets.

▶ **Louder and Slower Won't Help:** Teach Students to Help Their Readers Speak the Same Expert Language by Explicitly Teaching New Words

Teach writers to use a variety of strategies to help their readers understand new vocabulary. One way to do this is by adding new parts to sentences, or additional sentences after a domain-specific word.

If the purpose of research writing is to teach others, then expert vocabulary goes right along with it. Choosing which words to teach is often the easy part. If students worked to take notes and organize their understanding of new terms during their research, then they are well equipped to in turn reteach some of these same words to others. If it feels like their list is miles long, then you might ask them to choose the terms that feel most important to know, the ones most sources use.

One place to start is demonstrating how you can choose a word, write it in a sentence, and then either add the definition after a comma or in a new, second sentence.

Definitions feel best when—like all of your students' teaching-through-writing—they come from the writer's own understanding, not just a recopied dictionary definition. For example, with a fourth-grade class I could say:

> "I decided that the word incisors is really important to know when talking about rats, because so much of their survival depends on their big front teeth and they are also the things that get them into so much trouble, when they damage walls and wires and other things in buildings.

> "So, I wrote incisors at the top of a slip of paper, and I want to experiment with how I will define it. Now, I have to remember that I am an expert on this topic; I do not have to rely on someone else's definition for this word, because I already know. I studied it. I am going to teach people about this word just as I would any other fact. One way to do this is to think about a sentence or sentences to use the word in, almost pretending that everyone knows what this word means. Then when I actually write it down, I'll stop right after the word to add its definition between commas. Watch how I do this.

> "I could write something like 'Rats can chew through so many hard surfaces with their incisors. They can chew their way right through things like wood and concrete, and eventually even wear down steel!'

> "Now, when I go to write this down, I'll stop right after the word to define it. I'm going to explain what the word means, not just open a dictionary and copy it. Watch:

> > *Rats can chew through so many hard surfaces with their incisors, the four long teeth at the front of their mouths they use for gnawing. They can chew their way right through things like . . .*

> "Researchers, do you see how I did that? When I wrote I stopped right after the new word to teach it. Let me show you something quickly. I could do the same thing not with a comma, but with an additional sentence. This is especially good if I want to say a lot about the new word. I'm going to try this experiment again, on a new slip of paper. Then in the end I can decide which one I like the best. Watch when I write this way how I repeat the word I am trying to define in new sentences. (See Figure 4–5.)

> "The second sentence allowed me to say more. It helps your reader know you are defining a word when you repeat it near the start of the new sentence."

I could then invite students to try out another term from the class topic I am demonstrating with. Again, the important thing here is that I am showing a few possibilities, which gives me opportunities to teach students to make more thoughtful and more independent decisions.

Figure 4–5 My Demonstration Teaching-Through-Writing

Word: incisors

Rats can chew through so many hard surfaces
with their incisors. Incisors are four long teeth at the
front of a rats mouth that it uses for gnawing.
The incisors are curved, like claws, so it can scratch
and scratch a surface.

DEVISING TEACHING THAT MATCHES YOUR STUDENTS

• More Experienced Researchers May Benefit From:

More experienced researchers can learn to write embedding context clues. It is an
experienced skill, but one that many higher-level published nonfiction texts rely on
sometimes more than other techniques—a variation on the "add a second sentence"
theme. Teach students to think of what they know about the term they are teaching
and then write several sentences where they "show" but "don't tell" the definition
outright. For example, you could demonstrate by writing: "Rats chew through many
hard surfaces with their incisors. Wood, iron, and concrete all need to be continually
bitten and worn down to break through, but they can do it with time. Their jaws are
strong enough to support the continued pressure, and the sharp, curved shape of
their incisors make this gnawing easy work."

• More Emergent Researchers May Benefit From:

More emergent researchers can study a structure of many of the nonfiction texts they
have read. Borrowing techniques from these texts, for instance, students could bold
new words in their own writing and then place both the word and its definition either
in a text box or in a separate glossary at the end of their text. Again, be sure students
teach using their own understanding of words and do not just rely on looking these
up. The biggest hurdle is their misunderstanding of what you are looking for. If you

clarify that you value their definitions more than ones they grab from somewhere else, it is far more likely they will give this a try.

• Using in Content-Area Classes:

In a content-area research, students most likely came across several different variations of terminology for approximately the same fact (see "You Say Tomato, I Say Heirloom Jubilee Tomato Cultivar: Teach Students to Notice Variation and Gradation in Domain-Specific Vocabulary" in Chapter 3, p. 54). Teach your students that when they experiment with teaching-through-writing, they can keep similarly grouped words together and share those similarities with readers. In Sally's example of terms for wolf species, she wrote in one group, "There are many species of wolves, one of them is called Canis Lupus. There are many different kinds of wolves in the Canis Lupus species . . ." and in another she wrote, "The other type of species is called the Canis Rufus. The Canis Rufus means Red wolf, but their color is a mixture of black, gray, and reddish brown . . ."

• Additional Strategies:

Writers also teach important terms through repetition. Teach your research writers that essential terms should be purposefully revisited over the course of their writing. The art of this is to define the term when it's first introduced and then afterward rely more on context to remind readers of its meaning. Just as anything gets better with more practice, readers become more comfortable with the words we teach them if we give them many chances to experience them.

Reflecting on Student Growth

As students practice turning their notes into teaching, continually assess both the content they are writing about and the ways they are teaching-through-writing. Expect that as they learn new strategies they are trying them out and with practice using them with more ease. Continue to remind them to think of their readers. If they chose a specific audience, help them keep that reader or readers in mind while they write (see "I Feel Like We Have Met Somewhere Before: Teach Students to Find a Unique Focus for Their Research by Considering Their Audience" in Chapter 2, p. 19). Above all, encourage a great deal of experimentation, trying out multiple ways of teaching-through-writing even for one set of information.

As you assess the quantity of strategies students are using, the quantity of teaching-through-writing experiments students are trying, as well as the quality of those experiments, keep in mind Katherine Bomer's call to action in her book *Hidden Gems: Naming and Teaching from the Brilliance in Every Student's Writing* (2010): "We should give the same amount of time, respect, and attitude of inquiry into the mystery in our students' writing that we would give to a published novel, poem, or feature article. Yes, we notice misspelled words, and absolutely, we trip over sentences that don't flow in conventional, logical patterns. But we have decided to take a different stance: to notice the surprises, the brilliance, and the unique tone and signature style of even the most plain or scrawny or meandering piece of student writing" (p. 135). There is a way that our ever-moving school year can turn us into rigor and accountability fiends, but we have to make sure that we do not lose sight of the achievements taking place all around us.

To practice reading in the way Katherine is reminding us to, let's practice with an excerpt from Ruben and Julian's piece about what eagles eat. Ask yourself what strategies these students are trying, and more importantly, read with "the same time, respect, and attitude of inquiry" you would with other published texts. Think about what you can learn from them that you might teach others:

> **"The Eagle is a very beautiful bird but their eating habits could help you or even be dangerous to you. The <u>diet</u> or eating habits of an eagle could help you because it could eat and rid your house of mice and rats, but it can be dangerous for you that it eats ducks because that means you can't eat that and that it could rid the world of ducks and put them to <u>extinction</u>!!!!!**

> **"The eagle has similar eating habits to many different animals. For example the eagle and the bear both eat fish. The eagle is also similar to the owl because they both eat mice. The eagle is <u>similar</u> to many other birds because they both eat snakes."**

After reading this, looking for possibilities, I think I could teach other students to:

- Be honest with your readers. Help them see how a topic is often complex and can be both good and bad, or helpful and harmful, or fair and unfair.

- Help your reader see how a topic could have immediate importance in their lives.

- Experiment with different comparisons, because each can serve a particular purpose.

- Decide on words you want to add to the glossary, perhaps not just particular to that one topic but words that will be important to any related study as well.

Writers never stop developing, so we need to be mindful that we are celebrating that development all along the way. It not only supports further development, it can provide you with many teaching points you never imagined. With care, we can help students move from writing about research that feels like recopied notes to teaching-through-writing that is filled with the voice of a budding expert.

CHAPTER 5

Free from Graphic Organizers

Teach Students to Craft Organizing Structures with Their Readers in Mind

Ask nearly any professional writer what the hardest part of writing is and you may be surprised by the answer. Yes, coming up with ideas can be tough. Yes, crafting a story can be difficult work. But, often the most mentally challenging, the most strenuous process is: finding a structure. Whether it be a novel, a picture book or play, a poem, essay, or article, the thing that keeps one up at night—reworking, reworking, reworking drafts, going back and forth with editors—is the structure. Once you have found that magic formula, writing is a snap, but until then almost all of your writing and energy are put into that challenge.

Structure defines genres. When Lucy Calkins and my colleagues at the Reading and Writing Project set out to write the expansive *Units of Study for Teaching Writing* series (2006), they decided one key highlight would be structure. In studying reams of student writing during the preliminary research for the books, Lucy noted, "Many students were focused primarily on using writerly craft and reading-writing connections to 'pretty up' their texts with fancy beginnings and endings, sound effects, sensory details . . . But far too many of the pieces were structured in such a hodge-podge fashion that it seemed as if the writers were worrying about door-knockers on homes that had no foundation or walls!" (2006, p. 24). Any homeowner or *House Hunters International* aficionado knows that structural problems are reason number one to walk away from a sale.

Think, now, how much importance we give—or *don't* give—to structure. Sure, we do care an awful lot about it. An essay is not an essay without a "five paragraph" little hamburger we have all taught at some point in our careers. Though this is precisely the issue: we often *tell* students how to structure their writing, instead of *teaching* them how to do so on their own. We say, "You will write an essay, it will have five paragraphs, each paragraph will have six to eight sentences . . ."

Also, consider how much time and thought your students spend on structure across their research process. In the early days of my classroom it was often quite rare for students to look again at it once it was established. Often, I would have them make outlines in some shape or form near the start of a writing unit and then have them mostly stick to that plan, plodding forward to fill it in. Any revisions to the structure were often either quite small, or the ideas changed but the general organization did not. Four sections remained four sections, just with different words.

I am not suggesting a full-on revolt over teaching thesis, supports, and examples. We need that. Everything in informational writing is based on that nested hierarchy. I am suggesting, in addition, that we give structure more of its due, that we tie it closely to teaching through writing, that we encourage much more experimentation and problem solving throughout the process, and that structure is not just found through outlines and planning; it comes through writing, stopping to rework, then writing some more. While devising structure can be time-consuming and brain-frying, it is also surprisingly fun and invigorating to figure out just what system will best place your information in the mind of a reader.

This chapter will help you teach your students to choose structure for a purpose. If college and career readiness is our goal, then it is important to recognize that usually the reasons for writing may be assigned by a professor, or manager, or client, but the structure often is not. Even more important to have in mind is that in our increasingly global economy it is innovation that is most rewarded—the person who can find a newer, clearer, more effective, and more interesting way of doing something is lauded. Which means we need to give them strategies, and then be open to students rethinking and transforming them.

DEVELOPING HOW
Students Structure an Entire Piece

You cannot really know how to get somewhere until you first know where you are going. Instead of telling students how to organize their research writing at the very start of the unit, as in "You will write an essay, the first paragraph will be about the causes of the American Revolution, the next will be about . . ." or "You will create a nonfiction picture book, it will have five sections, the first section will be . . . ," teach them to consider that the way they organize their information is as important as how they write about it.

If you are especially daring, this can even lead to students selecting their own genres to match their varying topics and teaching. The Common Core State Standards expect that as students develop strength with writing they "begin to adapt the form and content of their writing to accomplish a particular task and purpose" (p. 18). Yes, you heard that correctly, they adapt "the form." So, consider that while more emergent researchers might need some time to study specific genres, as they grow and develop across grades we should allow more choice and should teach into that decision process. Appendix A of the Common Core State Standards opens up those choices quite broadly:

> *Informational/explanatory writing includes a wide array of genres, including academic genres such as literary analyses, scientific and historical reports, summaries, and précis writing as well as forms of workplace and functional writing such as instructions, manuals, memos, reports, applications, and résumés. As students advance through the grades, they expand their repertoire of informational/explanatory genres and use them effectively in a variety of disciplines and domains. (p. 23)*

That final line, "they expand their repertoire of informational/explanatory genres," reminds us to make sure we are not keeping our students within only one type of writing their whole career. Year after year, project after project, should not just be essays alone. Students have truly mastered an understanding of structure and genre when they can choose to use both for a purpose, not just do so because it has been assigned.

When deciding on strategies to support your students, consider if you will study particular genres or provide choice. Help them to experiment with the organization of their piece, to attempt quick drafts and then revise their plans, and to design their introductions and conclusions.

Differentiating Instruction for Organizing Entire Pieces

Teaching
for more
experienced
researchers

Decide if you will study one genre or allow some choice, then study examples of published pieces together, including those sources they have already collected. Teach students to sort and group their teaching-through-writing to find structures that work for their pieces.

Support students in studying published examples from a variety of informational genres, teaching them purposes for each. Teach students to group ideas in order to devise a structure early on, then throughout drafting and revision return to revise or redesign all in an effort to make their information clearer.

Teach students to keep their readers in mind as they choose a genre and structure to write within. As they draft and revise, teach them that writers constantly return to structure and wonder if there is a new form that would make their teaching clearer, or if their writing in a form is helping them narrow or change their focus.

Teaching
for more
experienced
researchers

Teaching
for more
emergent
researchers

▶ ## When I Grow Up I Want to Be Just Like You, Too:
Teach Students to Experiment with Structure by Studying Published Texts and Sorting Their Ideas

Teach students to choose a genre and structure that will best teach readers. One strategy is to teach them to go back through their teaching-through-writing experiments and practice grouping related information in different ways.

If students' teaching-through-writing experiments have been done on strips of paper it can be fast work to practice shuffling and reshuffling these sets, trying out different ways to group information and organize those groups. If instead notes and teaching have been done within notebooks, then you may need to teach students to code their notes in order to consider how ideas best fit together or simply mentally sort them.

You could ask, "Why not just make an outline?" Perhaps that would be useful, but the goal here is not to make one plan and then try to fill it in; instead, if we are to help our students independently craft structures that *teach*, then most likely we want to provide them multiple opportunities to practice and experience different ways of sorting information. It is worth a note, as well, that even *A Manual for Writers of Research Papers, Theses, and Dissertations* (7th edition), the gold standard of research style manuals, suggests that college- and adult-level research writers shy away from traditional outlining and instead make their early plans sortable, what they refer to as a "storyboard": "As opposed to lines on an outline, you can physically move storyboard pages around without having to print a new plan every time you try out a new organization. You can spread its pages across a wall, group related pages, and put minor sections below major ones to create a 'picture' of your project that shows you at a glance the design of the whole and your progress through it" (2007, p. 20).

When demonstrating this strategy, match the writing samples you are using to what most of your students have been creating—if they have been using slips of paper, you should come with a stack of prepared slips; if they have been using their notebook, then you should have some sample pages of a notebook. It is helpful to keep published texts on hand as well, showing students how you reflect on those when reorganizing your notes and teaching. It is really helpful to also have a chart prepared ahead of this lesson with ways of structuring texts and space to add more. In the example shown in Figure 5–1, I included the titles of published texts the class had already studied as reminders of those structures.

Figure 5–1 Charts for Experimenting with Structures

Published Texts Teach Ways to Structure Our Writing

Goal: To try ways of organizing our writing that published authors use

1. First, choose a text you admired
   See the chart for examples and look for your own.
2. Try to sort your ideas in a similar way.
3. When you finish ask two *important* questions:
   - "Do I think this will really help my readers learn about my topic?"
   - "What else do I need to learn or gather to use this structure?"

STRUCTURES IN (A FEW) PUBLISHED TEXTS		
Text	**Structure**	**Description**
"Most Likely to Succeed" by Malcolm Gladwell	Compare and contrast	Compared picking teachers to scouting football players
Cowboys on the Western Trail by Eric Oatman	Pretend story and factual information	Facts about cowboys in 1870s and pretend journal entries that tell a story
Snakes by Seymour Simon	Ideas grouped together	Each page or two is about another category of snake facts with one big picture, but no chapters or headings, like an essay.
The Kingfisher Atlas of the Medieval World	Chronological chapters	Most chapters are about an ancient civilization. Each goes in date order of what dates that group existed.
Oh, Rats by Albert Marrin	Pros and cons	Some chapters are about problems rats cause, others about ways they help or are very interesting.

With this chart and my examples in hand, you could demonstrate this skill with a class of eighth graders by saying:

"One thing teachers think about all the time is how best to organize our lessons—what we will do first, then next, and at the end. We try to order what we say and do so it's as helpful as possible for you, the learners. Nonfiction writers, because they are at-heart teachers, do the same thing. Researchers do not just teach information through the way they describe facts, they also do so through the way they order and organize their writing.

"Watch how I will first look over what I know so far—I have a bunch of strips of paper just like many of you. I'm going to sort them out to see which structure could best help my readers learn and hold onto this information.

"On this chart I listed a few ways of organizing information that we noticed in published texts. I'm going to first think about one that I admired, then try out sorting my information to see if it fits. Most importantly, before moving on, I'll ask two important questions that I listed at the top: 'Do I think it would really help my readers learn about this topic?' and 'What else do I need to learn or gather to use this structure?' Watch how I use these steps.

"I really liked that article by Malcolm Gladwell, 'Most Likely to Succeed' (2008). He was trying to teach how schools could find the best teachers, and he did that by comparing hiring teachers to scouting football players. I thought it was such an interesting way to organize writing: compare and contrast. Could I do that for my topic? Let me try it out. If I sorted these slips by compare and contrast . . . I know I have a few where I was comparing rats to something else . . . like this one comparing their jaws to people's, this one comparing their bodies to cats'. Now I need to ask both questions. 'Do I think this will really help my readers learn about this topic?' I think it could, if I found the right thing to compare rats to. I wasn't comparing all of these facts to the same thing. I also need to ask, 'What else do I need to learn or gather to use this structure?' If I wanted to do this structure I'd have to go back and not just use the same example each time, but also study that other topic more. Or maybe I could work with a partner, to share information with each other. Let me try another.

"*The Kingfisher Atlas of the Medieval World* (2007) was organized in an interesting way. It didn't just have random facts about ancient civilizations; it went in an order, following the years those groups existed. Let me try this one out. Can I sort these slips into an order or sequence? I think I could talk about rats when they are babies, then when they are older. Maybe things babies do, things older rats do. Yes, I really do think this could work. Remember, I can't end without asking, 'Do I think it would really help my readers learn about this topic?' The answer to this is yes, I think the sequence would help readers keep things in order and see that each stage of the rats' life is important. Then I have to ask, 'What else do I need to learn or gather to use this structure?'

"I'm going to stop there. I think you get the idea. I think about published pieces we have seen and try different ways of organizing my slips. I need to try out a bunch to see which would best teach my readers."

Making these plans could be fast work and will not take up an entire class period. That does not mean it is simple work; in fact, be concerned if your researchers stumble upon a plan immediately and feel they are "done." That might be a good indication that you should interrupt your class and demonstrate a few other ways to organize their writing, or probably more importantly, show them how you start to write within that structure, making a very fast draft of sections (described in the next strategy, "Like Standing in Front of the Dressing Room Mirror: Teach Students to Try On Their Structures for Size by Writing [and Rewriting] Quick, Brief Drafts," p. 95).

When a student named Vivien organized her essay on vegetarianism she tried out a few structures and ultimately found that the most compelling way to teach her topic would be in a cause-and-effect sort of structure, describing in the opening section what vegetarianism is and then in each following section grouping information into its effects, which she started to think of as creative subtitles that could go inside an essay or editorial. She created these not just by sorting, but with very specific audiences in mind: her mother, and the larger meat-eating world. She said, "I myself want to go vegetarian, but unfortunately I am not in total control of my life right now and my mom won't let me. But I'll show her and all of the meat-eaters of the world, meat doesn't equal survival!" She ended up with these groups of information:

- Section One: I Am Not a Nugget, the effects of vegetarianism on animal rights

- Section Two: A Healthier You, the effects on diet and health

- Section Three: The Green Diet's Going Green!, the effects on the environment

Her mission led her to organize her information in ways she thought would be most clear and most compelling.

DEVISING TEACHING THAT MATCHES YOUR STUDENTS

• More Experienced Researchers May Benefit From:

Invite more experienced researchers to innovate approaches to structure, by using their own published texts as well as combining different structures. A student deciding to write a research journal report, for instance, should collect a few actual professional journal articles but could also study magazine articles and episodes of informational television programs or online videos, blending a journal's use of subheadings with a television program's use of surprising comparisons.

• More Emergent Researchers May Benefit From:

More emergent researchers may think of their piece as having a table of contents, a strategy that schools working with the Reading and Writing Project have often found helpful. Teach students to jot quick "tables of contents," where each "chapter" will eventually become a paragraph or section. They can think, "What are the main categories or groups of information for this topic?" and then list these, going back at the end to pick the few they think are most important. They can ask themselves, "What are the categories for . . . ?" Expect your students to make a few drafts of this list, not just write one and run with it.

• Using in Content-Area Classes:

In a content-area study students often fall into the trap of trying to tell everything there is to know about a topic. To counteract this, you might teach students to look for a small part of the larger topic. Some areas are particularly fruitful, like roles (such as "women during . . ." or "teachers during . . ."), technology ("the development of transportation during . . ." or "changes in how genetics has been understood . . ."), supporting structures ("the role of mitochondria in . . ."), or even perspectives that appear to be less discussed ("Great Britain's perspective during the American Revolution . . .").

• Additional Strategies:

Students can also consider the genre for their piece. Sometimes it may be appropriate to assign this, but if we want our students to be independent with genre, we also need to provide some opportunities to experiment. In her first book, *Nonfiction Matters* (1998), Stephanie Harvey writes: "Genre and form are closely related to purpose. If a seventh grader is fed up with school lunches better suited to the postsurgery ICU, she might write a persuasive schoolwide petition . . . a class investigation into rain forest ecology could culminate in an environmental newspaper distributed schoolwide on Earth Day" (p. 168). Help students consider not just what is cool about genres, but also the purposes and audiences for each. If you are at a loss for options, Chapter 12 of *Nonfiction Matters* provides a very comprehensive list.

▶ **Like Standing in Front of the Dressing Room Mirror:**
Teach Students to Try On Their Structures for Size by Writing
(and Rewriting) Quick, Brief Drafts

**Teach students to try out their proposed structures by writing brief drafts.
One helpful demonstration is to teach them to write quickly and when
they feel stuck to make little notes to return to and move on.**

When you shop for clothes you never really know what to buy until you try things on—
when you see just how ridiculously that shirt fits you but (thankfully) how great you look
in that top and those jeans. It is the trying on that helps you commit to your purchase.
Trying on structure is no different. If left to it, some students could spend days and days
sorting and resorting slips of paper. Teach students to try brief drafts quickly (perhaps
even more than one version of the same points) to get a vision for how their writing and
thinking is progressing.

For example, when speaking to a class of sixth graders you could demonstrate how
you go from possible plans to quick drafts, assessing just how usable your plan really is
and what needs to be added:

"I want to show you how, even when you are just starting to get a sense of how you
could write, you can open up your notebook and try out some of your writing.

"I think the key, what helps me the most, is to write fast. If you feel stuck, just
make a little note and keep writing! I find that when I worry too much about
every single word—which, honestly, I really can get stuck doing—I slow way
down. Instead, act like you are in a race you have to win, and when you get
stuck it's just like you got to a hole in the ground, or a hedge, or some stones
in the road. You just have to jump over them and keep running. Watch how I
do this.

"I first remind myself of the way I thought I could organize my piece, then I pick
a part to start with, it doesn't have to be the beginning—actually it's easier to start
with one you know well—and how when I realize I'm not quite sure what to write,
I just make some notes and keep going, fast. Here I go.

"Remember, I was thinking this could be organized as a process with steps. I
thought I could write about baby rats and what they do and adult rats and what
they do. So let me take what I know, look at the teaching-through-writing experiments I already started. Here are the bunch I put together on adult rats and how

they get food. I'm going to look at these, then start writing. Okay, like a race, here I go . . . :

> *Adult rats need to find food for themselves and their babies. It can be hard for them to find food, though, especially because they like many things that we like. Most people can't stand rats and do whatever they can do to keep them away from our food. But* Oh Rats, *a book about how people and rats sometimes hurt and sometimes help each other, says, "Rats' bodies are built for survival." It's true, their jaws and . . .*

"Now, I can't find that paper that I wrote the facts about jaws on, and I think there are some facts about their teeth that I remember reading, but I don't know if I tried teaching-through-writing about them yet. I could stop everything and try to find all of that information now. But then I'd lose the race! So instead, I'm just going to write a note to myself, put a little star in the margin so I remember to come back to this, and then skip some lines and keep writing. Watch how it helps me keep going. (I then wrote in front of the class, as shown in Figure 5–2.)

"Did you see that? I'm writing to see if the structure I chose makes sense and will work. I also am making sure that I write as fast as I can. At any point I might want to stop, I just make a little note and keep writing."

Naturally, then, you might help students do a bit of goal setting to help them really measure just how much they are getting done. In *A Quick Guide to Reviving Disengaged Writers* (2011), I describe a number of ways to help students set goals and measure their growth, like setting a number goal of how many pages or lines they will write, or how many different sections or types of organization they will try. Or marking their page with a dot and an "x" of where they are starting and how far they hope to get within a short amount of time.

When our vegetarian crusader, Vivien, sat down to write about facts in her second section she was able to see just how clear and useful her organizing structure was. (See Figure 5–3.)

Figure 5–2 My Demonstration Quick Draft

Adult rats need to find food for themselves and their babies. It can be hard for them to find food, though, especially because they like many things we like. Most people can't stand rats and do whatever they can do to keep them away from our food. But on Rats, a book about how people and rats sometimes hurt and sometimes help each other, says, "Rats bodies are built for survival." It's true, their jaws and

find slips with those facts!

Check sense of smell

Rats can gnaw through wood, concrete and even metal. Imagine you are a rat and you can smell it, but you can't get to it. You would probably

Figure 5–3 Vivien's Quick Draft of an Essay Section

Some say that meat is a necessary part of your diet because it contains many important nutrients to help your body grow and flourish, such as iron, zinc, vitamin B-12, and many more. I agree that meat has its advantages and a vegetarian diet may be lacking the nutrients found in meat. However, that isn't the end of the world because there are plenty of vitamins and minerals found in all kinds of food, not just meat. For example, vitamin B-12, which helps produce red blood cells, is an important vitamin found in meat. According to kidshealth.org, vegetarians can get vitamin B-12 from "fortified soy milk and fortified cereals". Omega-3 fatty acids are also another important feature found mostly in fish. You can get omega-3 from foods such as "algae, some plants, and nut oils" (umm.edu). Sometimes, certain vitamins and minerals are most abundant in meat, so even though there you are getting the nutrients you need, that doesn't mean that you are getting an adequate amount. Therefore, some vegetarians take supplements to fulfill the daily amount necessary. Humans can get all the nutrition they need from plant-based foods without the fat and cholesterol contained in meat.

It appeared that grouping health concerns about vegetarianism into a section seemed to click, and the information she wanted to include flowed well.

DEVISING TEACHING THAT MATCHES YOUR STUDENTS

• More Experienced Researchers May Benefit From:

More experienced researchers will benefit from writing a bit within one structure, then switching to another one they were using to sort their ideas. In this example I could have tried out compare and contrast as well, grouping ways humans do things and the ways rats do things—such as how a human would just open the cabinet, pick up a box of cereal, and pour it in a bowl, while rats have a much harder time at getting food and yet have adaptations that help them. Additionally, teach these students to evaluate their drafts with the same key questions described in the previous strategy.

• More Emergent Researchers May Benefit From:

More emergent researchers may find it helpful to not jump straight to drafting, but instead line up their teaching-through-writing experiments in a grouping and order that makes sense and then write new slips (or notebook entries) that fill in the gaps between. They might construct a draft in pieces, before moving to write everything together as one. This has the double benefit of not letting those experiments disappear and also allowing them to physically revise their structure over and over before committing.

• Using in Content-Area Classes:

In a content-area study there are some genres and structures with particular importance to understanding different fields of study. In the sciences, for example, lab reports feel essential; so do journal articles that detail both the process of a study and conclusions. In a Social Studies study of civics or current events, students have some practice writing letters, speeches, or memos from their research, to both general and specific audiences. Introduce students to some of these genres, perhaps demonstrating how you try out these structures with your own information.

• Additional Strategies:

Devising structure also comes from anticipating the needs or point of view of an intended audience. You can teach students to think or jot about their audience's needs or point of view. It helps to consider a few questions: What will my readers be expected to do with this information? ("I want them to be kinder to rats, so maybe each section should be more about myths and facts about rats.") How much knowledge might they already have about this topic? ("I want to write for readers who don't know very much at all, so maybe making comparisons would actually be more helpful for them.") How do I get people interested in my topic? ("Yes, I think for sure I should write about myths, most people will be surprised what they learn. Just like I was.")

▶ **Ladies and Gentlemen, Boys and Girls:** Teach Students to Write Introductions *at the End* of Their Research Process

Teach students to write introductions—as well as conclusions—at the end of their research process. One strategy is to write an introduction that previews a main point from the beginning, middle, and end of a piece.

Think of how you introduce yourself and others in formal occasions—colleagues meeting your partner at a gathering, or someone you have to introduce before they give a speech, or even when you introduce yourself to a future employer through a cover letter. In each instance you draw on what you already know: "This is Sara. She teaches fifth grade at my school and we ran the school play this year." Introductions, though giving someone new a sense of things, come from what you already know. The same holds true for introductions to research writing. While they are inviting someone new to get to know your topic, though they come first, they should not come before you know what you are going to say to your readers in every other part of your writing.

I know I used to first and foremost teach students to make thesis statements and introductions (yes, with "hooks"). From there they worked to fill the rest in. The trouble is, when students write this at the outset they often feel boxed in, and we all know how they feel about revising. Instead, when you wait until students are quite far in their process, almost nearing the end, just before being ready to share it with others, their introductions and conclusions are far more purposeful and much better connected to what they were writing.

Because your students may be writing within a variety of genres, look back to published pieces. An abstract at the start of a journal article has a particular sound to it, whereas the starts of nonfiction trade books can vary. Conclusions go different ways in different genres.

The Common Core State Standards leave expectations for introductions and conclusions quite broad. In fact, for most of their schooling students are only expected to "introduce a topic"; "previewing what is to follow" does not come up until seventh grade. Conclusions, then, need just be "related to the information or explanation presented," and in middle school they should be statements or sections that "follow from and support the information or explanation presented." In other words, good teaching can help students far exceed grade-level standards for these two elements.

When students write introductions to research pieces, quite often they treat them as they do essays, letting you know each subtopic they will discuss. The problem, however, is that in essays there are often two or maybe three supports, but in research writing they can often have many more subtopics. What results (and it's actually quite endearing to see their attempt at applying a skill from one genre to the next) is a huge laundry list of subtopics pretending to be an introduction:

A growing sense of unfairness led the colonists to take action and demand independence from Britain. First, the Navigation and Molasses Acts raised taxes. Then, a proclamation stopped the colonists from going West. Then the Sugar and Currency Acts made the colonists even more upset. Then the Quartering Acts . . . Then . . . Then . . .

Instead, if students want to use the introduction strategy of previewing what is to come, teach them to think of writing introductions as a studio might when creating movie previews. A good preview, that is. For a class of fourth graders you might demonstrate by saying:

> "You know those previews that come on before a movie? The ones that get you interested in something that isn't out yet? You hear that voice, 'Next summer . . .' and then you see a couple scenes and hear some description, 'It began like any other summer, when . . .' Sometimes they make you want to run out and see that movie the day it comes out. Sometimes though—the bad previews—tell you almost too much. I'll sometimes turn to my friends and say, 'Well, now we don't need to go see that, we just saw practically the whole movie!'
>
> "When we write our introductions, we have to think about how to make a preview that makes people want to keep reading, but doesn't give too much away. One way to do this, just like how movie studios sometimes plan previews, is to think about all the main points—all the biggest points you make—and the most surprising facts. Instead of listing every single point, we just give some key ones from the beginning, middle, and end. For example, in my writing about rats, I have to think of the main points. I realize there are many. Turn to someone next to you and just quickly list together all of the main things you know I have been working on teaching . . .
>
> "Wow, there are a lot, like maybe ten big points. Instead of listing all ten, I'm going to say a few main ones from the beginning, middle, and end. If there is a surprising point that I think will make people want to keep reading, I might include that. Like I should start with the surprising fact that rats are a lot smarter and can do a lot more than people think. Let me try:
>
>> *Many people either think rats are disgusting and terrible or they try not to think about them at all. Rats are actually a lot smarter and can do a lot more than people think.*
>
> "Now, I'll list a few big points, from the beginning, middle, and end, not everything:
>
>> *. . . a lot more than people think. Baby rats learn to do things adults can do very quickly, even the way their appearance changes fast. When a rat learns to care for itself, its body allows it to find food and protect itself. As adults, rats can do everything from gnawing through concrete to surviving a long fall.*

Rats are a lot more social and loving than people think and often people can do more to hurt them than they do to hurt people."

This becomes a memorable analogy to return to as students write about their research. You can say, "Are you writing one of those previews that tell too much?" and a student will know just what you mean. Drawing connections from the way they structure essay introductions is helpful, while also being a point of differentiation for varying genres.

DEVISING TEACHING THAT MATCHES YOUR STUDENTS

• More Experienced Researchers May Benefit From:

More experienced researchers could be taught to consider what information readers will need to successfully read and understand the rest of their writing. For example, is there a specific term that readers should be taught from the very start? Or are there misconceptions they may hold that need to be questioned before proceeding? An introduction can be much more than just a catchy "hook" or a preview for what is to come; it can get a reader ready to learn.

• More Emergent Researchers May Benefit From:

More emergent researchers could be taught to begin their research writing with compelling narratives, perhaps even using one they experimented with already (see "Don't Just Say the Shark Swam, Bring It On and Let It Swim: Teach Students to Include Narrative Elements in Their Research Writing" in Chapter 4, p. 68). This is especially useful in setting a particular feeling or mood for their topic. Teach them to think of this as helping their reader experience a part of this topic before reading, like letting them observe ocean life swimming around a coral reef or stand in the room as the Declaration of Independence is about to be signed.

• Using in Content-Area Classes:

In a content-area study, student researchers will most likely not be covering all there is to know about a particular topic—either because they have learned to focus their writing or by the sheer probability that they will not have done the same level of exhaustive study as a graduate student might. Whatever the case may be, you may teach students to indicate what in their piece they are covering and what they are not. They could say, for example, "While genetics is a vast topic, still filled with areas of controversy, this paper will look specifically at . . ."

> **• Additional Strategies:**
>
> Conclusions vary just as much as kinds of introductions. Some that you might notice in published texts include: a call to action ("We must help our planet by . . ."), discussion of the future of the topic ("As technology moves forward, it will be even more important to . . ."), or making the point of view of this piece clear compared to others ("While some may say . . ."). In shorter pieces conclusions may recap main points, though just as in the movie-preview analogy the focus is on central ideas, not on covering small details.

DEVELOPING HOW
Students Structure Within Sections

Teaching your students to create their own overarching structure, the general outline or plan for how their entire piece will go, is a big risk, for sure. But with your guidance and their practice, it will pay off for both the piece they are writing and their understanding of research writing in the future.

If they have already tried to take facts and experiment with how they will teach them, those slips of paper or jots in their notebooks have already brought them a long way from just regurgitating what they read to really writing from expertise. You may have found that these slips, along with their structure plans, have made their writing stronger than before. You also, though, may have found students listing teaching-through-writing experiments one after another, or others just writing quick drafts that felt disjointed or rambled a bit. Teaching overarching structure is important, but to have really cohesive, rigorous writing, we need to also teach how to structure writing within sections.

The Common Core State Standards expect this as well, that students can "link ideas within," and sometimes even "across," "categories of information." For older students they use the term "cohesion," meaning basically the same thing. Great teaching connects concepts, examples, and ideas together; great research writing does the same.

When teaching your students to develop structures within sections of their writing, decide on the kinds of organization you will demonstrate, how you will remind them to consider their readers, and the types of words and phrases you will teach them to use to connect ideas.

Differentiating Instruction for Organizing Within Sections

Teach students to look for a logical order or sequence for their information within sections, trying out different ways with their readers in mind. Help them to supply linking language to go from one idea to the next.	Demonstrate for students how you experiment with section structures just as you have with the overarching structure. Teach them to think of how they want their readers to progress through their writing and to supply phrases that provide that guidance.	Teach students to structure the sections of their writing, perhaps even repeating structures across sections of their piece, all with the needs of their audience in mind. Support students in gathering and using phrases that connect or clarify differences between ideas.	**Teaching for more experienced researchers**

Teaching for more emergent researchers

▶ Rearranging Your Sock Drawer: Teach Students to Thoughtfully Organize Ideas and Details Within Parts

Teach students to structure not just the main topics of their writing, but also to thoughtfully organize ideas and details within parts. One strategy is to consider overarching structures as ideas for smaller sections as well.

Just as a whole text has a structure, so can the parts. Whether they are sections or chapters or just paragraphs, the order in which you arrange your ideas and details has an impact. In published research, writers use a variety of techniques to organize their information. What tends to matter most for our research writers is that they are taught to be aware of how they are organizing their bits of teaching-through-writing, that they do not just plunk them down in any order.

Help your students see that ways of organizing entire pieces are often not so different from organizing small sections or parts. If you look back to the chart in Figure 5–1 (p. 91), many of those structures (and others you add with your class) can be used again on a smaller scale. It helps to first consider which section or part you will be writing within and what type of organization might help a reader understand that subtopic best. Then, see how the writing you have tried already can fit and what more you need to add.

For instance, if you were demonstrating by writing about the Boston Tea Party you might have sections like, "British Actions That Angered Colonists," "The Colonists Organized a Dramatic Response," "The Event," and "The Immediate Aftermath." When getting to a section on the aftermath of the event you might look back to "Charts for Experimenting with Structures" (Figure 5–1) and say:

> "While these were ways that entire published pieces were organized, we can borrow these same structures for smaller sections. Like in this section I'm working on, I'm planning to write about the immediate aftermath of the Boston Tea Party. I have a bunch of teaching-through-writing experiments, but I'm not really sure how to put these in order. So let me think. Could I make a compare-and-contrast structure to this section? Maybe compare the colonists' responses to those of the British? That could work well. Maybe a pretend story with factual information? That might be interesting, like a fictitious letter about someone who participated or observed.
>
> "I can take the bits of writing I have already done and organize them within one of these structures, then decide what more I will have to write or revise to see if it fits."

Here, too, is a time to bring in not just text but visuals or other media (see "A Picture *and* a Thousand Words: Teach Students to Carefully Select Visuals to Support Their Text" in Chapter 4, p. 78). Students can use these text structures to arrange their writing into text features, like charts or diagrams that compare and contrast. Myrah, Moniba, and Sanna, a group of students researching penguins, organized some of their information they had on the similarities and differences between common birds and penguins into "Compare" and "Contrast" text boxes. (See Figure 5–4.)

Figure 5–4 Compare and Contrast Text Boxes

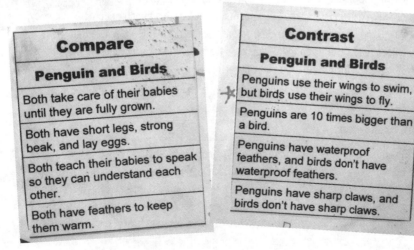

They found a way to make key distinctions that will help their reader learn about penguins, and did so in a streamlined form.

DEVISING TEACHING THAT MATCHES YOUR STUDENTS

• More Experienced Researchers May Benefit From:

More experienced researchers can be taught to experiment with a repeating structure, one they mostly stick to but can bend at times when needed or for effect. Teach them to do some quick jotting of their plan and then quick drafting to see if it will work across more than one section. Jotting a plan like "start with a fictional story, then information, and have a timeline on almost every page" or "subheading for each part, describe the new step in time the section is about, write a myth, then give facts against that myth."

• More Emergent Researchers May Benefit From:

More emergent researchers may benefit from learning to consider order or sequence within their writing. Teach them to first see if there is already an inherent sequence to their information (such as dates or a process). If not, help them consider what order will be most helpful for their readers to learn. Sometimes big concepts should come before smaller details or basic information should be learned before moving to variations and more complicated ideas. As they think through this, teach students to lay out their writing in different orders until they find one that makes sense to them.

• Using in Content-Area Classes:

In a content-area study, to further support students' focus on using their writing to teach, you might open up your planning a bit and talk to them about the ways you organize lessons for class. Show them how you have a bunch of content you could cover and how you consider the content, your audience (in this case: them!), and what you hope to teach them. You keep these three things in mind as you make decisions about the information you will select, the order you will place it in, and even the language you will use. Help your students connect this to the thoughtful choices you and they can make while writing.

• Additional Strategies:

Teach students to not just attempt to find a structure that works with the information they already have collected, but to also let a good structure be their guide for additional research. Demonstrate choosing a structure for a section—like compare and contrast—and then realizing that you do not have enough information to write. Show students that you do not just toss out this plan; instead you might open your notebook and see if there are facts you just have not tried teaching-through-writing yet, or perhaps create a two-column chart: "What information I need" and "Where I think I can find it," listing several facts you need to find, and sources, both those you have already read and ones you think you could find.

▶ **Go Two Blocks and Take a Right:** Teach Students to Use Phrases That Link Ideas and Guide Readers' Thinking

Teach students to use words and phrases that help readers transition from one idea to the next. One way is to group phrases based on their effect on readers' thinking and choose with these effects in mind.

Once our students have a structure to work within, they need to learn to guide their readers through the structure. Instead of just listing cause-and-effect relationships, it helps readers to write, "While that one event had two major causes, it had many different effects. One was . . . ," so they can follow your thinking.

The Common Core standard 2c is specifically for language that connects ideas, and it details how this language should get increasingly more complex. For instance, in fourth grade the CCSS provide words like *another, for example, also, because,* where in fifth grade it becomes *in contrast, especially.* For older students they expect that words do not just link ideas but "create cohesion and clarify relationships among ideas and concepts," that is to say, that words both connect and separate ideas.

One way to teach this is to teach students not just phrases, which would be easy enough to post up on a list, but their functions. I will often group these and then attach a visual, like arrows or road signs, so students can consider what they want this reader to be thinking and how these phrases can help. (See Figure 5–5.)

For a class of fifth graders I might then demonstrate using these phrases by saying:

"As we have been talking about, it's important that when we write we don't just record everything we know, but help our readers really learn from us. We even have to teach our readers how to move through the structure we are creating, to really follow our thinking from one idea to the next. Watch how when I'm writing, I stop to think, 'What do I want my readers to do next?' and then I write a phrase to help them move in that direction.

"Here is a chart of some phrases, with some road signs we can post while we write. You probably know a bunch of other phrases you could use as well. Let me

Figure 5–5 "Phrases that Link Ideas" Chart

Phrases that Link Ideas
Goal: To direct your readers' thinking while they read

Phrases that "Move Forward" (from One Idea to a Similar One)	
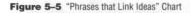	For example . . . In addition . . . Another . . . Also . . . First . . . then . . . then . . . That is to say . . . Another way to say that is . . .
Phrases that "Turn A Corner" (from One Idea to a Different One)	
	In contrast . . . However . . . Alternatively . . . This is different from . . .
Phrases that "Give Directions" (Tell Readers How To Pay Attention)	
	Notice how . . . There are three main points, first . . . Consider this when you realize that . . . Look at the picture to the right . . .

try this out. I'm writing this section of my piece on adult rats and the amazing things they can do. I'm going to write a sentence or two and then stop to ask myself what direction my readers should go in next. I'll start with:

Rats use their many senses to survive.

"Now that I wrote that, I need to decide if my readers should move forward and turn a corner, or if I need to give them directions—tell them to watch out for something or read with something in mind. Well, if I wanted them to read forward I could use a phrase like one of these:

Rats use their many senses to survive. For example, according to "Whisker Wonders," a PBS Science Bytes episode, rats' whiskers work in a similar way to humans' hands. That is to say, they help them precisely feel and understand what they are touching.

"What if instead I wanted my readers to pay attention to how many facts I was going to give, because I have many? I could have written instead:

Rats use their many senses to survive. Three parts of their body are most essential . . .

"If I keep writing I might want to clarify how rats have similar senses to people, but they use them differently. Like when I'm talking later about seeing things I could say:

In contrast, rats cannot see very well at all. While you can see a piece of bread lying on the floor, rats would see a very blurry image and would have to use their other senses.

"Do you see that while I write, I need to ask myself what I want my readers to do next? I can then use phrases and words to help them. Almost like I am leaving road signs for them to follow."

After a demonstration like this, you might ask students to work briefly with a partner to add to one of the paragraphs you started or instead to talk out one of their own paragraphs. Help them focus most on thinking about their readers and how the phrases they choose help to orient their learning.

DEVISING TEACHING THAT MATCHES YOUR STUDENTS

• More Experienced Researchers May Benefit From:

More experienced researchers should be encouraged to add to this chart with their own bank of phrases. One way is to go back to published pieces to analyze words and phrases authors use and the effect they have on readers, a strategy that supports both writing standards and reading. Beyond written texts, students should be encouraged to listen to television news shows and documentaries as well as listen carefully to everyday conversations, jotting down phrases they hear that they could use in their research writing.

• More Emergent Researchers May Benefit From:

More emergent researchers may benefit from physically manipulating these phrases just as they might be sorting and arranging their teaching-through-writing on slips of paper. One version of this is to have phrases on cards that a student can try placing between two slips and then jotting off of. Another version is to have cards that they "play," almost like a game, organized in groups similar to the chart. As they are writing, they stop and draw a card from the pile that matches the direction they want their readers to go in, testing out the word or phrase to see if it works.

• Using in Content-Area Classes:

In a content-area study often students are writing about one small piece of a much larger topic; therefore they will need to learn not only the strategies described above, but also language to reference larger ideas and topics simply and effectively. They will need to connect ideas not just within a section, but across sections, and even with the larger study of history or science outside of their piece. They will need phrases like, "Directly resulting from," "This is in contrast to," "Within the study of," "Referring back to," and so on.

• Additional Strategies:

As your students write, new categories may come up, for example phrases that make you stop and take notice, such as "Especially . . . ," "Above all . . . ," "Barring all else . . . ," perhaps symbolized by a caution sign. Perhaps there are phrases that summarize or help readers reflect, or ones that help a reader make a clear visual image. You may want to take some of the phrases I placed within the same category and put them in their own, like one category for sequencing information. In the end, the way you organize phrases should match your students' understanding and the analogies you use within your classroom.

Reflecting on Student Growth

As students study and practice ways to organize whole pieces and within sections, expect that they will learn and practice a wide variety of strategies and show greater control and sophistication in the way they organize their writing. Look for students making clear decisions about how their ideas and information will be grouped together.

If students are to truly develop independence in research skills, you should not be the only one assessing their progress. Teach them to reflect on their own work and make decisions about next steps. One way to do this is to have students look back to charts you have made, mentally checking off strategies they have tried and those they have yet to try.

For instance, look back to charts from this chapter and imagine they were hanging them up in your classroom—such as Figure 5–1, "Charts for Experimenting with Structures," and Figure 5–5, "Phrases that Link Ideas." You could ask students to have out their jottings and drafts, and talking with a partner, use their finger to "check off" in the air strategies they have been experimenting with and "circle" those they still want to try.

You may find it helpful to create additional charts that not only show *what* students can try but can help students assess the *quality* of their writing. Perhaps posting some student examples of well-organized sections or including some "tips" on charts, such as:

- "Strong organization makes sense to a reader, sections that build in importance or follow steps. You could help your reader understand even more by carefully choosing titles of subsections."

- "Do not only use linking words within a section to go from idea to idea, but also think about how your language can help your reader remember ideas you already stated, and either add in or compare the new information you are teaching them."

With your support, your students can become more independent in developing organizing structures within their research writing, letting go of the need for teacher-created graphic organizers and instead writing purposefully to reach their readers.

CHAPTER 6

Without Agonizing Memorization
Teach Students to Cite Sources on Their Own

I once spent an entire forty-five-minute period in a fifth-grade classroom just trying to have students make sure that in their bibliographies they put the author's last name first, then a comma, then the first name, then a period. I am not kidding. And I wasn't even the only adult in the room! There were four other fifth-grade teachers in the classroom with me. We modeled, we conferred, we huddled, we modeled again, we had partners check in with each other, we modeled again, we were exhausted. By the end of the writing period we looked at each other and said, "Well, we still have copyright date, title, and publisher left . . . That should only take seven more weeks."

Citations are a necessity. That we can agree on. Making things is very tough work and people who make new ideas, products, and artistic experiences deserve credit. It is a labor of love, but labor nonetheless, and everything that is created involves risk, time, and the challenge of balancing life and career. Citing someone's work and ideas is not just a "school thing," it's a form of thank you for the time someone spent to give you the gift of a new idea. And of course, it's illegal to plagiarize; though I think that provides more fear for college students who are at risk of expulsion than for our younger students (though, a little overdramatic storytelling never really hurt anyone, right?).

The other important aspect of citation is that it provides invitations to readers. A works-cited page is actually a series of invites: "I think you would really love to read this book," "And this article is so critical to understanding this topic," "And I would never have read this other article had someone else not told me about it"; this is really what the writer is implicitly saying. I am a bit of a works-cited geek, I have to say. I read them obsessively and quite usually go find those other sources. At times I do it because I just want to learn, learn, learn, and I know the author picked those particular sources out of tons of others that were dropped. At other times I find it a great exercise in sleuthing, especially when someone who seems terribly important makes a claim. I like to see if what they *said* they read actually matches what was written—and there are many times when the two do not match up.

To teach students to cite well, we need to rethink the way we typically work. In *Plagiarism: Why It Happens, How to Prevent It* (2008), Barry Gilmore writes, "Many teachers address citation issues mainly by distributing to students examples (or directing them to an online site that shows examples) of proper citation . . . but a handout is not sufficient here; it doesn't clearly answer the when? or why? questions that the reasons for avoiding plagiarism [embody]" (p. 76). We must move away from handouts and rules to memorize and help students understand the many reasons for citation, but also how to become more independent in referencing sources. It need not feel like only an after-the-fact activity, but can instead be a part of the way they communicate with readers.

This chapter intends to help you teach your students citation work that is appropriate to where they are in their development as well as crack the code on practices that can make their learning about citation more purposeful and practical, so you don't have to run around the room saying, "No, it's a colon before the copyright date!" In essence, it's a way to avoid a repeat of that forty-five-minute period on the minutiae of name placement in a reference list.

DEVELOPING HOW
Students Cite Sources

Citations can take many forms: in-text citations, footnotes, endnotes, works cited (or the mutually confusing gray area of "works cited," "bibliography," and "references") and probably others I do not even recall that my twelfth-grade English teacher will be disappointed I forgot.

I think it's less important which ones we teach and more important how we teach them, keeping in mind that the rules of citation are always in flux. The downfall of that forty-five-minute class period was that we were teaching citation as a finite set of rules to be memorized, instead of teaching students to *read* and *comprehend* citations' examples and explanations, just as we would teach them to read anything else.

We have to teach students *how* to figure out the rules for themselves, as a habit that they will carry with them through their lives and equally through all the revisions those rules inevitably go through. In fact, if we focus more on rule-memorization, there is a chance we are actually teaching the wrong thing. For instance, if you open up your old MLA style manual you will probably find that any website was supposed to be fully listed in the source, something like:

"*<http://verylongwebsitename.com/too/many/extra/words/to/ever /remember>*"

However, rules change as the world changes. Now when referring to the Web address, MLA style asks a writer to write this:

"*Web.*"

APA style, however, still would like the full address. And who knows, any and all of this may change again. If I am teaching students to memorize citation guidelines, there is a good chance what you taught will be outdated. We have to teach them to fish.

The last point about all of this is to consider what you assess to be developmentally appropriate for the growth of your writers. The Common Core State Standards try to lay out one continuum of development across writing standard 8, suggesting that below fourth grade students need not worry about citations, that fourth and fifth graders should "provide a list of sources," that sixth graders need to quote or paraphrase to "avoid plagiarism" and provide "basic bibliographic information," and finally, that from seventh grade on up, students should be able to follow "a standard format for citation." This is just one sense of how this could go. No doubt some fourth graders could do more; they really could provide basic bibliographic information, and some eighth graders will struggle a great deal with this standard and need teaching that scaffolds them up.

Differentiating Instruction for Citing Sources

Teaching
for more
emergent
researchers

Teach students to be aware of citations in published texts they are reading, to notice when and why authors tell you where ideas came from. Help students keep a list of very basic bibliographic information, as developmentally appropriate, even if just titles of books.

Assist students in evaluating what needs to be cited and what general knowledge often does not. Teach them to decide when a citation is also necessary for effect, such as linking a well-known expert to a quote. Teach them to include basic in-text citations and source lists whenever they quote sources.

Teach students to first be aware of the style required by their writing task (usually assigned by teachers) and to reference the appropriate guide online or double-check the accuracy of Internet bibliography creators. Help them study and use standard formatting for both in-text citations and source lists.

Teaching
for more
experienced
researchers

▶ **You Would Never Believe What He Said Next:**
Teach Students to Cite Sources Within Their Writing

Teach students that books, authors, and other experts can "talk" within their research writing and that the punctuation conventions of narrative dialogue can carry over to nonfiction writing.

Every student in a research study will need to turn their reading into writing in some way; it's the main point of teaching-through-writing. Therefore, it may make sense to study in-text citation first. Again, avoid teaching this as a set of finite rules. Instead, notice what published writers do and experiment doing the same. One effective place to start is to look at instances in which published writers directly quote. You could look to books, articles, websites, newspapers, or any place where the author allows someone else to speak in their writing.

When you model how to do this in your own demonstration piece, you might have a paragraph with information already included that you realize you did not cite very clearly, or you may instead have just the start of a paragraph already written and you will write more in front of your students, showing how you remember to cite while writing. When I have done this with classes that have already written narrative pieces at some point in the year, I will refer to this basic form of in-text citation in this way—in the following example I talk with a seventh-grade class:

> "This year we have been studying how dialogue in the novels you are reading reveals things about characters, and how adding well-crafted dialogue to your narratives brings readers into the internal, emotional life of the people you are describing. We have seen that allowing characters to speak—in the books you read and the stories you write—is essential to the experience readers have with any text.
>
> "It turns out, the same holds true for research writing. Having voices come out in your writing shapes the way your readers will learn from and react to your writing. I know you might be thinking, 'Am I supposed to have a character show up or something in this essay I'm writing about fault lines in the United States?' Not exactly. Instead, what I am saying is that the books and articles you've been reading and jotting notes on, those sources and their authors can—and actually should—speak within your writing.
>
> "Let me show you how I can use the exact same rules for adding and punctuating dialogue that we have been working on in writing, to allow sources and experts to talk within my research writing . . ."

When I demonstrate, I could show a published example of in-text citation that looks like dialogue, then try it out myself in front of students. It is often important to demonstrate a variety of ways to write the same sentence, like:

- *The book* Sharks *states, ". . ."*
- *The book* Sharks*, by Beverly McMillan, suggests that, ". . ."*
- *Beverly McMillan, an author and expert on sharks, says, ". . ."*

That mental image of experts "talking" inside of students' writing does a great deal to make the often-abstract concept of citation more concrete and palatable for our students. From this first, basic way of in-text citing we can support students in building more sophistication and nuance—all the while using the same steps of studying a published piece or pieces, then demonstrating in my own writing, and being certain to show a variety of ways to construct the same sentence.

DEVISING TEACHING THAT MATCHES YOUR STUDENTS

• More Sophisticated Researchers May Benefit From:

More sophisticated researchers should study other examples of in-text citation and style guides. For instance, APA style requires the addition of publication dates within the text. You could teach students these by first looking at professional journal articles. Most essentially, realize that for all of us following formal citation rules is a challenge. Share the strategies you use, for example, by referencing websites such as Purdue University's Online Writing Lab, lovingly referred to as the "OWL."

• More Emergent Researchers May Benefit From:

More emergent researchers may also need support in having a sense of when to cite and when not to. Let's face it, in a research study everything can feel like someone else's idea. While it's always a good idea to cite—and for our more emergent researchers they should probably overdo it instead of underdo it—a paper full of quote after quote shows little retention or personal thought. You may help them know that common knowledge—things that everyone who knows about a subject agrees on ("bees are insects," "dogs can be pets")—do not typically require citation. Specific statistics, surprising or unusual facts, or other ideas that a reader wouldn't typically know usually should be cited.

• Using in Content-Area Classes:

In a content-area study it can feel even more important to tell readers where information came from, noting if it was experimental data gathered by the writer or by some other experts' study—for example, if primary source documents are being quoted ("In his own letter to the President . . .") or if it is some scholar's interpretation of primary sources ("upon studying Elizabeth I's letters, historian Alison Weir noted . . .").

• Additional Strategies:

The way sources and authors are described and introduced to a reader by the writer has a big effect on the way that quote or paraphrase is received. Teach students to experiment with different descriptions within sentences before the quote is introduced or by using appositives (phrases set off by commas describing the subject before it), as in: "Sharks, an engaging and well-researched book overviewing everything you need to know about this often-misunderstood sea creature, states . . ."

▶ Crack the Code, Not Just Memorize It: Teach Students to Study and Apply Rules for Source Lists

Teach students to use standard formatting for citation lists. One strategy is to teach them to analyze formatting as if it were a code to crack.

While Internet-based bibliography creators are often very helpful, they are also imperfect, so an understanding of how to create standard citation lists is an important skill.

When I reflect on my experiences with citations in school, I find that it was often a combination of yellowed "Style Guide" copies from the school library, repeated "last name, comma, first name" directions said aloud, and piles of boredom. Creating a works-cited list felt as interesting as getting a flu shot. It doesn't have to be this way, though. Learning to read and use citation rules can, with a little bit of finesse, actually be kind of interesting.

One way to do this is to treat style guides just as they are intended to be handled, like a particular code, and turn it up a notch for student buy-in. Think about how odd they are. How much easier it would be to just write: "I read such-and-such book by so-and-so author, which came out in 2008." Instead, terms are flipped out of order, with periods, colons, or italics spread about. It truly is a code that people who understand the secret language find very helpful (as in, "Oh, good, here is that article by Richard Allington that the author mentioned. Having his last name first in this list helped me find it quickly . . ."). So take that conspiratorial note and raise the volume on it.

When teaching a class to study citation guides, I will first talk about code cracking and demonstrate how to crack a nonsensical code I made up. I will ask the students to try on another made-up code, and then, with sleight-of-hand, move to cracking a style guide's code. It is useful to have a chart in your classroom like the one shown in Figure 6–1.

With a class of sixth graders I might say:

"You know those lists of books at the end of some of the sources you have read? Like if I turn to the back few pages in this book, it's called a bibliography. I don't know if you know this, but the way they are written is actually a special, almost secret, code. A lot like how spies use codes with each other to communicate. If you know the code you know exactly what the message means and how to use it. Bibliographies, or works cited, or reference lists, are written in codes as

Figure 6–1 Things to Look for When Cracking a Style Code

Things to Look for When Cracking a Style Code

Goal: To study citation styles so we can use those codes ourselves

Look at a style example and ask yourself:

1. How many **parts** are there? *How many different kinds of information?*
See the chart for examples and look for your own

- For each part, what **kind of information** is it? *A name, a date, a place?*
- For each part, is there **punctuation**? *Periods, commas?*
- For each part, does it have special **formatting**? *Italics,* underline?

2. What **order** do the parts go in?

3. Try to put in your **own information** to test the code.

well. People who know how to read them find they are very useful, but to many people they are somewhat mysterious. Today, however . . . we are going to crack that code.

"Before we jump right to code cracking I first would like you to learn just what code-crackers might look for. Take a look at this chart with me. (See Figure 6–1.) We are going to read codes asking ourselves these questions—How many parts are there? For each part, what kind of information is it? Does it have special punctuation? Does it have special formatting? We'll then ask what order the parts need to go in. And last, to make sure we actually cracked the code, we will try to use some of our own information to test our skills out, to verify if we actually figured out the secret way of writing.

"To start, here are two codes I made up. The first I want you to watch me try to crack, the second I'll ask you to try. If it goes well and quickly, we will graduate to the ultimate spy code-cracking challenge. We will try to find the secret way of writing used on pages like this bibliography.

"Okay, here we go. Here is my code . . ." (See Figure 6–2.)

Figure 6–2 My Code Example

LEHMAN, Christopher! (Brown Hair)
black shoes; black pants.

"Watch how I ask myself each of those questions on the chart to try and crack the code . . ."

While demonstrating, I make a point of pausing to think aloud a bit, to weigh ideas. When doing this, it helps if I mirror some of the issues I am sure my students will come across. For example, I am fairly certain many will look at general types of information like, "Oh, that's a name," but won't study how individual parts are handled, so I want to mimic their potential pitfalls within this demonstration. Saying, for example, "Type? Well, I can see it's a name. Now, let me pause here a minute, I could just move on, but I have to make sure that I look to see if there are smaller parts of this larger 'name' section and how each part is handled. Yes, see, if I look more carefully, it looks like there is a first name and a last name listed. And they are not in the usual order . . ." With the above sample "code" the end of the demonstration could sound like:

"So let's see what our cracked code seems to be. I wrote down all of the parts, I think it's . . .

LAST NAME IN CAPITAL LETTERS, First name with just one capital! (Hair Color) shoe color; pants color.

"Now, to see if we really cracked the code, we have to put in our own information. Um, I need a volunteer I can write about . . ."

Next, I might have students try to crack a new code and test it out in partnerships. If my teaching was clear, it should take no more than a minute or two for them to try. Then we'll laugh a bit and I'll end the lesson with individuals cracking one more code, one standard citation from a style guide. Individuals can then check with a partner before working together to try and put one of their sources into the format.

DEVISING TEACHING THAT MATCHES YOUR STUDENTS

• More Sophisticated Researchers May Benefit From:

More sophisticated researchers should learn to read and analyze style guides in a similar fashion. Memorization alone is never the key to standard formatting—no one other than very gifted editors can do that, and even then they nearly always reference the most up-to-date guides. These researchers should be exposed to a variety of styles, and also learn to search for the format that matches their purpose. Multiple-author books vary to a degree from single-author journal articles, as both do from no-clear-author website pages. Knowing that a first step is asking, "What am I trying to find a citation format for?" is often good next learning for students who already show some flexibility with citation writing.

• More Emergent Researchers May Benefit From:

More emergent researchers may not be ready for full citation writing; your most essential task for these students is to make them aware of citations in published texts. When looking at published texts together, pause at points where authors cite and talk about them. Have them discuss why the author chose to mention another writer or source, and if they are ready for it, talk a bit about how they did this. "Did you notice that this author both explained where this quote came from and listed the page number? For me, it means that I can go turn to that page if I wanted, but it also makes me—as the reader—feel like this fact is very important because it came from an expert."

• Using in Content-Area Classes:

Content-area teachers, especially those of older students, may want to partner with their English Language Arts counterparts to decide how and when to select the type of style students should use. While most content areas are likely to use APA style, a grade-level team may decide to begin the year with MLA in all classes and then move to APA for all, in order to provide consistent practice. Or alternatively, decide to be clear with students on the different styles and to always use specific ones with the appropriate content.

• Additional Strategies:

Students almost certainly will need practice in locating bibliographic information in their sources, print resources often being easier than digital or media ones. On the one hand, the Internet is a very fast and often accurate (though not always) way of locating information. Just act as if you are going to buy a book from nearly any major site, and you'll find that publication date, publisher, and other information are readily available. You may also want to extend the code-cracking metaphor and do a few rounds of quick searching and pointing: "Okay, hand your book to the person on your left, now point to the . . . publication date! Hurry, find it! Check with your partner to see if they are in the right spot." A few fast rounds for repeated practice will go farther than a belabored and long explanation based on only your front-of-the-classroom example.

Reflecting on Student Growth

As students develop citation skills it would be simple enough to look merely for accuracy. In a way, this could be the easiest growth to track: either one has cited correctly or one hasn't. Case closed. If your feedback to students, however, is so simplified, then you may just end up perpetuating the challenges this chapter aims to overcome; you might once again be encouraging students to see citation as a "school" exercise and not a tool for communicating with readers. Therefore, do look for accuracy, but think of your conversation with students as one about reaching readers.

For instance, in Rosemary's essay on cell phone use in schools, she cites sources within her piece and includes a works-cited list. As you look at her writing, think of the strengths you are seeing and suggestions you could make to her. It might help if you phrase your thoughts with, "I notice when you are teaching readers you. . .". (See Figures 6–3 and 6–4.)

Figure 6–3 In-Text Citation

> Not having a cellphone like others might make students jealous, eventually leading to theft. Michael Kwan says, "Particularly when it comes to high school, young people can be very competitive, fighting for popularity amongst their peer group. This can manifest itself into stealing if a particular individual brings an especially expensive cellphone to school." Some might say that just because the students want to be popular, they wouldn't steal cellphones. However, in high school and even middle school, popularity is one of the most important things to a student. Kwan says, ". . . and they would do anything just for popularity. Stealing a phone is no big deal for them."

For Rosemary's in-text citation work in this paragraph you *could* say:

- "I notice when you are teaching readers you include the author's name with the quote because you want them to know who this person is. I would like to suggest that it is sometimes important to cite the publication or give some background information as well."

Or instead, you could talk as if the citations are a conversation with her readers and say:

■ "When readers, like me, see a name attached to a quote it makes the quote feel more important. It is like you are telling me through your writing, 'I have been studying a lot about this topic and I want to point you to someone you should know.' It makes your point feel more substantial. Can I suggest something as well? Because readers will be interested in knowing who *you* know within the expert world of this topic, could you also include a bit more about who they are or where the quote is coming from? It will not only make us feel smarter as your readers, it will also teach us where to go to learn more about this topic. For example. . .".

Figure 6–4 Works Cited

Smith, Charmayne. "Pros & Cons of Cell Phones in School." *EHow.* N.p., n.d. Web. 29 Nov. 2011. ⟨http://www.ehow.com/about_5393195_pros-cons-cell-phones-schools.html⟩.

Kwan, Michael. "Cons of Cell Phones in School." *lovetoknow cell phones.* N.p., n.d. Web. 29 Nov. 2011. ⟨http://cellphones.lovetoknow.com/Cons_of_Cell_Phones_in_School⟩.

With this example in mind, think about how you would talk to Rosemary about her works-cited page. Your conversation can be just as warm, especially when you think of it as giving her tips for communicating with readers. When double-checking formatting you could talk about the fact that readers have expectations for how these pages go, so they can go and find those sources themselves easily. When talking about the sources she chose or checking that all are included, instead of just saying:

■ "You must have two books, one Internet page, and one interview cited . . .",

you could instead say:

■ "Your readers, like me, look at works-cited pages not for formatting, but for ideas. They want to see which authors they should know, which books are important on this subject—basically your works-cited list becomes sort of a recommendation list. So you want to look at it and ask yourself if it feels like it

makes the best recommendations possible. For instance, when I was considering which sources I should cite, I. . .".

It is a much different conversation than the usual mundane, task-driven one. With your
support, your students can learn how to make decisions about citations, to understand
and use style guides, not just feel they must memorize rules, and to see these skills as
another way to craft their writing to teach readers.

CHAPTER 7

English or Content Areas,
Long Studies or Short Projects

Turn Strategies into a Study That Matches the Needs in Your Classroom

As you heard in the first strategy in this book, I love to cook. I always have the goal of dazzling family and friends with a new recipe. A dinner guest is like a challenge to outdo what I've done before. To this end I watch—rather, *obsessively* watch—any food program I can find (the rise of the Food Network was like the heavens opening up). I watch slightly interested in the recipes, but mostly interested in the tips and techniques: the unusual spice blend, the way to roll and julienne basil, parchment paper baking bags and tented foil steamers. I jump from show to show, technique to technique, building a mental storehouse of cooking strategies. Then comes the afternoon before a dinner guest, the moment I get to put it all together, choose from my arsenal, deciding which new things to try and which familiar things to continue with.

Now for you, as you close the cover and step away from this book, the time has arrived: company is coming. Now is the time to take all of the strategies you have dog-eared or jotted beside and decide how to turn those strategies into studies that will outdo what your students have done before.

The first consideration is what type of study to prepare. The Common Core State Standards offer two general structures to consider; writing standard 7 expects that students will be able to "conduct short as well as more sustained research projects" (p. 18). Each has its own purposes and possibilities.

You plan a long, formal dinner with friends to allow for a lot of face time: you get to gossip, laugh, worry about each other's love lives, kids, or jobs. At a dinner party you expect several hours to share in others' company and perhaps the prospect of getting to know some newer faces that much better. Long research studies offer students that same sort of long time to savor: to learn many different strategies, to have a lot of time to practice, and repeated opportunities for your input.

A short research project, then, could be akin to quick lunches with a friend whose schedule is just as busy as yours. You meet out "somewhere fast" or have her over for "something quick" because you both have a million things to do but you haven't seen each other in so long. You use that opportunity to reconnect with someone you care about, even if the time is short, and especially if you have not seen each other for a while. The short research project can be squeezed within other teaching you are busy doing; it is a way you can remind students of strategies you do not want them to forget and a chance to add newer, more rigorous teaching as the year moves on.

In my view, short research projects generally will have the most bang for their buck if they have come after a longer study. This longer study would not necessarily need to have happened within the same subject area as the shorter ones, or even the same month, but scheduled as a follow-up to more greatly studied strategies. Organizing in this way will allow you to reinforce and further develop skills. That being said, a long study is certainly not a prerequisite and any practice with research skills is better than no practice at all. Just be realistic in your expectations; a small amount of practice may not yield what a greater amount of practice can. Aim for short studies to refine specific needs, long studies to develop larger habits and skills over time and practice.

The Four-Course Dinner: Plan a Long Study of Research Reading and Writing Skills

At the start of *The Art of Teaching Writing* (1994), Lucy Calkins begins with these words: "If our teaching is to be an art, we must draw from all we know, feel, and believe in order to create something beautiful. To teach well, we do not need more techniques and strategies as much as we need a vision of what is essential. It is not the number of good ideas that turns our work into art but the selection, balance, and design of those ideas" (p. 3). At heart, teaching is most effective when it is responsive to students, their interests and needs. Your study of research skills will pay off the most not because you use every strategy, in order, but because you select and balance with your students firmly in mind.

One essential piece of the plan is helping your students see a logical pace within your teaching. I recall early in my career when my day-to-day teaching was driven more by the cool workshop I attended the day before or the lesson I saw my friend down the hall teaching. It felt exciting to me to try something new, but upon reflection I'm sure it was disjointed to my students. One framework for planning is to build upon the writing process most students are familiar with. Think, if you are hosting a long dinner party, you do not have to struggle with how your menu will progress; instead, you think inside of a typical flow to plan your dishes: appetizers, a salad, main meal with sides, and end with dessert. Educators often have different words for the writing process, but typically it follows its own typical flow: begin by collecting writing ideas, then rehearsing those a bit, then drafting, next revising and editing, and finally ending with publication. Having a logical organization helps students better internalize independent writing habits, and it gives a mental place-holder for your teaching. In fact, when the Carnegie Corporation performed a meta-analysis of numerous studies on writing instruction, they found that using a "process writing approach" and teaching "writing strategies" were highly effective practices to increase student writing achievement, so much so they joined their short list of suggested best practices for all students in grades 4 to 12 (*Writing Next* 2007). The CCSS are equally on board, expecting students to "develop and strengthen writing as needed by planning, revising, editing, rewriting, or trying a new approach" (p. 18).

So begin with the writing process as a framework, have your students in mind, and then choose strategies—pull those strategies from this book, other sources, and your experience—that will help them develop strength in research. Figure 7–1 shows one example of how this could go.

Notice how you could use this book's chapters more or less in order, keeping in mind that learning is not just about always moving to the new, new, new idea; it is also about returning to ideas to work through them a bit more. So as you move across the process you may return to strategies you have already "covered" but you now want your students to become more independent in using. There is also ample room for more teaching beyond this book. Perhaps during the reading and note-taking phase you teach students that while reading nonfiction it helps to have conversations; you read differently because of those conversations, as described in *Navigating Nonfiction* (2010) from the *Units of Study for Teaching Reading* series. When you help students edit their writing, you may pull out your copy of *Catching Up on Conventions: Grammar Lessons for Middle School Writers* (2009) to figure out how you will approach both subject-verb agreement and moving your students from an informal to more formal style. Equally, the standards see the "Research to Build and Present Knowledge" strand as necessary for all types of

Figure 7–1 Organizing a Long Research Study

	COMMON WRITING PROCESS STEPS	WHAT THIS COULD LOOK LIKE IN A RESEARCH READING AND WRITING STUDY	SOME POSSIBLE STRATEGIES FROM THIS BOOK
Collecting	Gather many topics so you can find the one with the most potential. Allow one idea to lead you to the next.	Instead of being assigned a specific research topic, brainstorm many. Begin reading sources, gathering a variety of notes, even if you do not in the end use them all.	Chapter 2 Pages 12, 16, 24 Chapter 3 Pages 38, 42, 46, 51, 55
Rehearsing	Try out ideas, weigh possibilities before committing to the best ones. Experiment with your writing: imaging possible structures, possible starts and ends, possible details to include.	Experiment with ways of teaching-through-writing, possible structures and even genres, all with the purpose of helping readers learn. Perhaps returning to sources for notes when you notice holes in your information.	Chapter 2 Page 19 Chapter 4 Pages 64, 68, 75, 78 Chapter 5 Pages 90, 104
Drafting	From experiments, commit to a structure and ways of developing ideas through writing. Aim to write quick drafts that you know will not be perfect, but that you can always return to or try again.	Choose a genre and structure and write quick drafts to try them out. Draw on teaching-through-writing experiments you have tried, though instead of simply recopying, rewrite experiments but also write in new ways.	Chapter 4 Page 72 Chapter 5 Page 95
Revising	Making large, brave changes. Not just "fixing what is wrong." Reworking the structure, details, and so on, all to better connect your readers with your intended meaning.	With your readers in mind, reread and ask if you are teaching in the clearest way possible: clarify examples, reordering sections. Help your reader follow your thinking, and so on.	Chapter 4 Pages 78, 81 Chapter 5 Pages 90, 99, 104
Editing	Making sure the words on the page match what you are trying to say so your reader understands your meaning.	Editing for clarity of text and graphics. Keep your readers in mind, making sure they can learn from the piece you are creating.	Chapter 4 Page 78 Chapter 5 Page 107 Chapter 6 Pages 116, 119
Publishing/ Celebrating	Allowing your writing to be seen by others, to feel that your life and ideas are valuable and worth sharing.	Using your writing to teach others, to help them become more of an expert just as you have. Aim to share work beyond the classroom.	

writing, including narratives. Best-selling novelists and poets research just as judiciously as informational writers. So while this book was largely focused on expository writing, you could partner many of these strategies with great narrative writing companions like Katherine Bomer's *Writing a Life: Teaching Memoir to Sharpen Insight, Shape Meaning—and Triumph Over Tests* (2005). Certainly you will sit back and think of your students' reading and writing work from the months before this one, and ask yourself which teaching made them engage like never before and which tough stuff you still want to hatch solutions for. To teach well is to see the great wide world of strategies and methods through the eyes of your students.

The Quick Lunch: Plan Short Projects to Check-In and Extend Independence

Short projects will have the most traction if you see them as a recharge along students' development, the way over a plateau, the point between where students currently are and where the standards want them to be. It would be simple enough to just do as the CCSS ask; in upper elementary the expectation is that students do short research projects that "build knowledge" and in middle school that they conduct slightly more refined versions that "answer questions." It would be simple enough, and probably engaging, to just jump into interesting topics and try to answer compelling questions. Why is the sky blue? Let's go look it up. Where did football come from? Quick: go search and then let's make a quick timeline. Think, though, of all of the standards as woven together, not as separate tasks to "do." Think of standard 6 as complementing all of the other research work across the standards, and remember that short projects can both check-in on skills and add new strategies to the mix. With some finesse and some responsiveness to student needs, these quick projects could go from fun exercises, to fun exercises that really support student achievement.

So, then, once again begin by planning with your students' needs in mind.

Plan Short Studies to Reinforce Prior Teaching and Learning

One way is to reflect on prior teaching and build from there. For instance, if your students have already studied ways to take notes—either with you or a colleague earlier in the year—you might find that come winter they seem to have forgotten what they were taught. (Gasp! When would that *ever* happen?) You might plan a short study that primarily aims to remind and provide additional practice with note-taking. You might plan for two or three days to reteach a strategy they know and maybe add in a few new ones. Because this study is quick, know that you probably would not end up with new writing—at least not a polished piece, but instead you would expect that from the start to the end their note-taking would improve. You could string together some strategies from Chapter 3 in your planning, such as:

- Slow and Steady Wins the Race: Teach Students to Paraphrase Well by Pausing to Think (p. 38)
- On Your Mark, Get Set, Go: Teach Students to Make Smart Choices About When to Use Which Type of Notes (p. 42)

and

- Without Lists to Memorize: Teach Students to Revise Their Notes to Include (and Learn) Domain-Specific Vocabulary (p. 51)

While planning, it will help focus your class to give them a larger, heftier goal than just "let's take notes better." You could begin by highlighting that chapter's goal of note-taking to develop expertise by saying: "I want to help you study the way you learn and support you in developing ways of taking notes that will help you become experts."

Plan Short Studies to Address Newly Uncovered Student Needs

You could also plan short studies based on needs you are uncovering, not just looking for evidence of prior teaching. Perhaps you are noticing that many of your students' final projects at the end of a unit sound very similar. You find yourself falling asleep to the blur of paper after paper that sounds like it is regurgitating your notes from class or the readings you have assigned. You could plan a short study to give students practice with strategies that could help them take ownership of their research writing.

For example, you might begin first by checking that you are not assigning just *one way* their writing should go, but instead teaching students skills for developing their own research. In *Nonfiction Craft Lessons* (2001), JoAnn Portalupi and Ralph Fletcher caution: "beware of going back to the time when teachers assigned every fourth-grade student to write a state report . . . give them as much choice as possible within that common topic. That way each student can find her own angle, or rope off her own area of expertise that is distinct from the other sources" (p. 110). To help students break free from just sounding like the textbook, you could plan three or four days to teach them strategies for narrowing down to a focused topic and writing some quick drafts about it. You may not expect, then, that their writing will be superbly revised, as that is not your purpose for this study. Instead, you could expect that they learn ways to find their own topic inside of a larger one and that they try out a few ways to write with their own voice. For instance, if in Science your students have been studying ecosystems you could choose a lesson from Chapter 2 to teach them to narrow their focus: "I Feel Like We Have Met Somewhere Before: Teach Students to Find a Unique Focus for Their Research by Considering Their Audience" (p. 19). You might tweak the lesson a bit to show how you think of your audience's interests and which ecosystem they might find most interesting or which part of that ecosystem they would want to know more about—like perhaps your cousin would find the tundra fascinating because he loves winter and winter sports and would be interested to know what can survive and what can't in that biome. Because you are aiming to do this project quickly, your students most likely would not be reading new information on their topic (except maybe for homework); instead they might review teaching and sources you have already shared with them to practice writing in a new way. So you could choose a writing strategy or two from Chapter 4 that will pump up their quick writing while staying within your short window of time: "Don't Just Say the Shark Swam, Bring It On and Let It Swim: Teach Students to Include Narrative Elements in Their Research Writing" (p. 68) or "Push Beyond Paragraph-Shaped Recopied Notes: Teach Students to Write from Their New Expertise with Their Notebooks Closed" (p. 72).

Short Studies Need Short Projects, and More Importantly, Vice Versa

Of course these examples are only that—examples. Student needs are numerous and so too are potential responses. Continue to plan by starting with needs, choosing strategies to address those needs, and *then* designing a study to engage them and their work. (See Figure 7–2.)

Then, the final consideration in your planning is that students will need something to be taking notes on, so the glue that could bind a short *study* together could be an engaging "short *project*." There seem to be two ways to go with this: one is you might direct a study's focus, giving students some texts within a narrow topic to read. Say, your Social Studies class is studying the westward expansion in the United States, and so you gather a few sources for students to read on its impact on Native American communities. The other way could be that you invite students to develop their own topics to study. In *Comprehension & Collaboration: Inquiry Circles in Action* (2009), Stephanie Harvey and Harvey Daniels describe such searches as "mini-inquiries" that are initiated by teachers' and students' own questions and skepticism. In Chapter 8 of their book—which is a treasure

Figure 7–2 Organizing Short Research Projects in Response to Student Needs

Student Needs	Strategies to Draw On	Possible Short Study
My students would benefit from additional experience in making their writing feel specific. Right now it sounds a bit vague or informal.	Chapter 3's strategies on learning vocabulary (pp. 51 and 54). Chapter 4's strategies on teaching vocabulary through writing (p. 81).	Perhaps focus a study on learning and using expert vocabulary. This could include going back to revise writing they have already completed or trying to use expert vocabulary in conversation.
I would like my students to give speeches or presentations, but I worry that they will be disorganized because their writing sometimes is unfocused.	Chapter 5's strategies on organizing an entire piece (starting on p. 88). Chapter 5's strategies on organizing within sections (starting on p. 103).	Perhaps focus a study on organization. They could use notes they have already taken from class or instead prepare on-the-fly talking points from videos on controversial topics. Your teaching would focus most on helping them make initial structures and going back to revise them.

trove of examples of these sorts of studies—Stephanie modeled for a fifth-grade class by sharing her own curiosity about everything from "Is Tide [detergent] more expensive just because it is Tide?" to "Is recycling without sorting as environmentally sound as separating recycled items?" (p. 146). She then showed students how she quickly searches for sources online and talks with others to develop answers. Stephanie was not teaching about Tide detergent (though I did learn a valuable shopping tip from her); she was teaching students a process of learning and strategies they can use to get to answers.

Always keep in mind: the "project" is what will drive student engagement, but the carefully chosen teaching is what will ensure students develop stronger and stronger skills. The Common Core State Standards are not expecting that students just *do* short and long research projects, and to just assign time would be missing the opportunity to support students in meeting the research reading and writing expectations within the entire standards document.

Crafting Seasonal Menus: Make a Yearlong, Subject-Wide Plan to Energize Students and Meet Key Standards

The power of your instruction, regardless of the type of study you undertake, comes from your making decisions based on student work. As John Hattie writes in *Visible*

Learning: A Synthesis of Over 800 Meta-Analyses Relating to Achievement (2008), "I discovered that feedback was most powerful when it is from the *student to the teacher*" (p. 173), that seeing students' writing and reading as feedback to your teaching—what they have found the most useful, what they are still confused by, what they are not yet aware of—is what drives student development. His review of research suggests that what we say to students is only half as important as what their work is saying to us.

The final day of any study, any project or notes or speech or essay, is not the end. It is not just loading the dishwasher and putting away the glasses. Instead, the last day of one study is the first day of the next. It is thinking about how the potatoes would have been even better with some rosemary and maybe you should try chocolate sauce on the cake next time. This can be the way research skills develop within your own class, or even more effectively, how they could live within your entire school.

To make the greatest impact, think of long and short studies as a story that unfolds across a student's school year, each chapter building upon the last. My colleague at the Reading and Writing Project, Mary Ehrenworth, often suggests that you should sit down with any other teacher your students will learn from during a year to plan out purposeful ways curriculum unfolds. For instance, if you and your colleagues choose to look at research skills as one area to plan across a year, you could decide when long and short studies could move in sequence from content area to content area, in order to provide much-needed practice and ever-increasing rigor. (See Figure 7–3.)

In this example, students may take on a long three-week research study in Social Studies sometime in the fall of the school year, learning not just about a historical time period but also learning research strategies across a process. Then, shortly after that, students could have a short study in Science to reinforce note-taking skills—and so on,

Figure 7–3 Pacing Long and Short Research Studies Across the Year

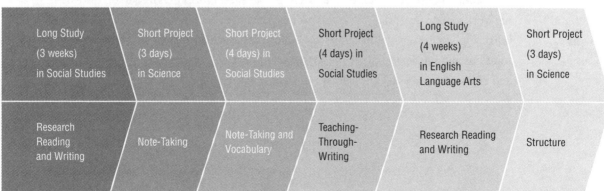

Long Study (3 weeks) in Social Studies	Short Project (3 days) in Science	Short Project (4 days) in Social Studies	Short Project (4 days) in Social Studies	Long Study (4 weeks) in English Language Arts	Short Project (3 days) in Science
Research Reading and Writing	Note-Taking	Note-Taking and Vocabulary	Teaching-Through-Writing	Research Reading and Writing	Structure

helping students see skills across contents and hosting a year of learning that develops independence. From this initial plan, the focus of any project would be tweaked from the one that came before.

If, for instance, Social Studies and Science are taught by different teachers, then at the end of the initial research study those two teachers may email a bit with one another. The Social Studies teacher could sum up: "I think students did a good job with this unit, but I noticed two areas they really could use more practice in. We were right to predict note-taking, but in particular most found using a range of notes challenging. Also, they really loved trying to write anecdotes; if you can work that in I think they'd love it, like maybe there is a way to make that fit with note-taking . . . maybe as a kind of reflection." Students would surely benefit from such a thoughtful approach to curriculum.

An Invitation to Energize

Greater independence, more energetic research, meeting key standards; these do not need to be thought of as mutually exclusive pursuits. I hope, instead, our work together through these pages has helped you feel that each can fuel the other. When you allow students opportunities to independently practice strategies, you are able to assess and make decisions about their research needs. The expectations of the standards can be an invitation to develop new teaching, not just a burden to grapple with, and students become more independent because you plan for their development with skills and standards across a study and across a year.

My sincere hope, as well, is that you have taken the title, *Energize Research Reading and Writing*, as not just a call to enliven the work of your students—that this is not just an aim to get students to meet standards and pass tests—but that in the process of studying your students and the teaching of research, you also feel more energized to do the essential work you do every day. I love this profession of ours because at its core it is so deeply nurturing intellectually. Challenges are opportunities, and when we are grappling with solutions and one finally clicks, the feeling is unmatched. We give energy to our students and often, sometimes when we least expect or really need it, they energize us in return.

APPENDIX

Looking Between the Standards and These Strategies:
A Conversation

To be honest, I get a little nervous listing strategy "correlations" with standards in a handy-dandy chart. Textbooks, workbooks, and educational software often love to slap a "meets standards" sticker on their products as if they are the sole solution to achievement. The truth is only *you* can help your students "meet standards"; your work in balancing ideas, reflecting on student progress, and being in an ongoing conversation about your teaching. So think of these charts as a part of that conversation.

LOOKING BETWEEN THE *READING STANDARDS* AND THE STRATEGIES IN THIS BOOK

	KEY IDEAS AND DETAILS			CRAFT AND STRUCTURE			INTEGRATION OF KNOWLEDGE AND IDEAS			RANGE OF READING AND LEVEL OF TEXT COMPLEXITY
	1	2	3	4	5	6	7	8	9	10
CHAPTER 2	X	X	X	X	X	X	X	X	X	X
Investigation Starts with "I": Teach Students to Find Their Own Research Topics—Because They Will Have to Eventually							X		X	X
But What if They Want to Research Unicorns or the Cure for Baldness?: Teach Students to Let Available Sources Select What Is Possible to Study							X		X	X
I Feel Like We Have Met Somewhere Before: Teach Students to Find a Unique Focus for Their Research by Considering Their Audience						X	X		X	X
I Know Because Your Voice Goes Up a Little When You Lie: Teach Students to Look for Signs of an Opinion Being Passed Off as a Fact	X		X		X	X	X	X	X	X
CHAPTER 3	X	X	X	X	X		X		X	X
Even Kindergarteners Are Taught, "Find the Main Idea": Teach Your Students to Rely on Understanding, Not Tricks, to Hold onto Large Concepts	X	X			X		X			X

(Continues)

	KEY IDEAS AND DETAILS			CRAFT AND STRUCTURE			INTEGRATION OF KNOWLEDGE AND IDEAS			RANGE OF READING AND LEVEL OF TEXT COMPLEXITY
	1	2	3	4	5	6	7	8	9	10
Slow and Steady Wins the Race: Teach Students to Paraphrase Well by Pausing to Think	X	X		X			X			X
On Your Mark, Get Set, Go: Teach Students to Make Smart Choices About When to Use Which Type of Notes	X		X		X		X			X
Scratch That, Reverse It: Teach Students That the Most Important Thing They Can Do for Learning Is to Revise Their Notes	X	X					X		X	X
Without Lists to Memorize: Teach Students to Revise Their Notes to Include (and Learn) Domain-Specific Vocabulary	X			X			X			X
You Say Tomato, I Say Heirloom Jubilee Tomato Cultivar: Teach Students to Notice Variation and Gradation in Domain-Specific Vocabulary	X			X			X		X	X
CHAPTER 4	X	X	X	X	X	X	X	X	X	X
When I Grow Up I Want to Be Just Like You: Teach Students to Study Published Texts and Borrow (or Steal) Effective Writing Techniques	X		X	X	X	X	X		X	X
Don't Just Say the Shark Swam, Bring It On and Let It Swim: Teach Students to Include Narrative Elements in Their Research Writing				X	X	X				
Push Beyond Paragraph-Shaped Recopied Notes: Teach Students to Write from Their New Expertise with Their Notebooks Closed				X	X	X				
An Ounce of Prevention: Teach Students to Look for Missing Information While Writing, Not Just After Drafting	X					X		X	X	X
A Picture and a Thousand Words: Teach Students to Carefully Select Visuals to Support Their Text		X	X			X	X		X	X
Louder and Slower Won't Help: Teach Students to Help Their Readers Speak the Same Expert Language by Explicitly Teaching New Words				X	X	X				

(Continues)

	KEY IDEAS AND DETAILS			CRAFT AND STRUCTURE			INTEGRATION OF KNOWLEDGE AND IDEAS			RANGE OF READING AND LEVEL OF TEXT COMPLEXITY
	1	2	3	4	5	6	7	8	9	10
CHAPTER 5	X	X	X	X	X	X	X		X	X
When I Grow Up I Want to Be Just Like You, Too: Teach Students to Experiment with Structure by Studying Published Texts and Sorting Their Own Ideas		X	X		X	X	X		X	X
Like Standing in Front of the Dressing Room Mirror: Teach Students to Try On Their Structures for Size by Writing (and Rewriting) Quick, Brief Drafts	X	X	X		X	X				
Ladies and Gentlemen, Boys and Girls: Teach Students to Write Introductions at the End of Their Research Process					X	X				
Rearranging Your Sock Drawer: Teach Students to Thoughtfully Organize Ideas and Details Within Parts			X		X	X				X
Go Two Blocks and Take a Right: Teach Students to Use Phrases That Link Ideas and Guide Readers' Thinking				X	X	X				X
CHAPTER 6			X			X	X		X	X
You Would Never Believe What He Said Next: Teach Students to Cite Sources Within Their Writing		X				X	X		X	X
Crack the Code, Not Just Memorize It: Teach Students to Study and Apply Rules for Source Lists							X		X	X
CHAPTER 7	X	X	X	X	X	X	X	X	X	X
The Four-Course Dinner: Plan a Long Study of Research Reading and Writing Skills	X	X	X	X	X	X	X	X	X	X
The Quick Lunch: Plan Short Projects to Check-In and Extend Independence	X	X	X	X	X	X	X	X	X	X
Crafting Seasonal Menus: Make a Year-Long, Subject-Wide Plan to Energize Students and Meet Key Standards	X	X	X	X	X	X	X	X	X	X

LOOKING BETWEEN THE *WRITING STANDARDS* AND THE STRATEGIES IN THIS BOOK

	TEXT TYPES AND PURPOSES			PRODUCTION AND DISTRIBUTION OF WRITING			RESEARCH TO BUILD AND PRESENT KNOWLEDGE			RANGE OF WRITING
	1	2	3	4	5	6	7	8	9	10
CHAPTER 2	X	X		X			X	X	X	X
Investigation Starts with "I": Teach Students to Find Their Own Research Topics—Because They Will Have to Eventually	X	X					X	X	X	
But What if They Want to Research Unicorns or the Cure for Baldness?: Teach Students to Let Available Sources Select What Is Possible to Study	X	X					X	X	X	
I Feel Like We Have Met Somewhere Before: Teach Students to Find a Unique Focus for Their Research by Considering Their Audience	X	X		X			X	X	X	X
I Know Because Your Voice Goes Up a Little When You Lie: Teach Students to Look for Signs of an Opinion Being Passed Off as a Fact	X	X					X	X	X	
CHAPTER 3	X	X					X	X	X	
Even Kindergarteners Are Taught, "Find the Main Idea": Teach Your Students to Rely on Understanding, Not Tricks, to Hold onto Large Concepts	X	X					X	X	X	
Slow and Steady Wins the Race: Teach Students to Paraphrase Well by Pausing to Think	X	X					X	X	X	
On Your Mark, Get Set, Go: Teach Students to Make Smart Choices About When to Use Which Type of Notes	X	X					X	X	X	
Scratch That, Reverse It: Teach Students That the Most Important Thing They Can Do for Learning Is to Revise Their Notes	X	X					X	X	X	
Without Lists to Memorize: Teach Students to Revise Their Notes to Include (and Learn) Domain-Specific Vocabulary	X	X					X	X	X	
You Say Tomato, I Say Heirloom Jubilee Tomato Cultivar: Teach Students to Notice Variation and Gradation in Domain-Specific Vocabulary	X	X					X	X	X	

(Continues)

	TEXT TYPES AND PURPOSES			PRODUCTION AND DISTRIBUTION OF WRITING			RESEARCH TO BUILD AND PRESENT KNOWLEDGE			RANGE OF WRITING
	1	2	3	4	5	6	7	8	9	10
CHAPTER 4	X	X	X	X	X	X	X	X	X	X
When I Grow Up I Want to Be Just Like You: Teach Students to Study Published Texts and Borrow (or Steal) Effective Writing Techniques	X	X		X	X		X	X	X	
Don't Just Say the Shark Swam, Bring It On and Let It Swim: Teach Students to Include Narrative Elements in Their Research Writing	X	X	X	X	X		X	X	X	X
Push Beyond Paragraph-Shaped Recopied Notes: Teach Students to Write from Their New Expertise with Their Notebooks Closed	X	X		X	X		X	X	X	X
An Ounce of Prevention: Teach Students to Look for Missing Information While Writing, Not Just After Drafting	X	X		X	X		X	X	X	X
A Picture and a Thousand Words: Teach Students to Carefully Select Visuals to Support Their Text	X	X		X	X	X	X	X	X	
Louder and Slower Won't Help: Teach Students to Help Their Readers Speak the Same Expert Language by Explicitly Teaching New Words	X	X		X	X		X	X	X	X
CHAPTER 5	X	X		X	X	X	X	X	X	X
When I Grow Up I Want to Be Just Like You, Too: Teach Students to Experiment with Structure by Studying Published Texts and Sorting Their Own Ideas	X	X		X	X		X	X	X	
Like Standing in Front of the Dressing Room Mirror: Teach Students to Try On Their Structures for Size by Writing (and Rewriting) Quick, Brief Drafts	X	X		X	X	X	X	X	X	X
Ladies and Gentlemen, Boys and Girls: Teach Students to Write Introductions at the End of Their Research Process	X	X		X	X		X	X	X	X
Rearranging Your Sock Drawer: Teach Students to Thoughtfully Organize Ideas and Details Within Parts	X	X		X	X		X	X	X	X
Go Two Blocks and Take a Right: Teach Students to Use Phrases That Link Ideas and Guide Readers' Thinking	X	X		X	X		X	X		X

(Continues)

	TEXT TYPES AND PURPOSES			PRODUCTION AND DISTRIBUTION OF WRITING			RESEARCH TO BUILD AND PRESENT KNOWLEDGE			RANGE OF WRITING
	1	2	3	4	5	6	7	8	9	10
CHAPTER 6	X	X		X	X	X		X		X
You Would Never Believe What He Said Next: Teach Students to Cite Sources Within Their Writing	X	X		X	X	X		X		X
Crack the Code, Not Just Memorize It: Teach Students to Study and Apply Rules for Source Lists	X	X		X	X	X		X		X
CHAPTER 7	X	X	X	X	X	X	X	X	X	X
The Four-Course Dinner: Plan a Long Study of Research Reading and Writing Skills	X	X	X	X	X	X	X	X	X	X
The Quick Lunch: Plan Short Projects to Check-In and Extend Independence	X	X		X	X	X	X	X	X	X
Crafting Seasonal Menus: Make a Year-Long, Subject-Wide Plan to Energize Students and Meet Key Standards	X	X		X	X	X	X	X	X	X

REFERENCES

Adams, Simon, and Kevin W. Maddison. 2007. *The Kingfisher Atlas of the Medieval World*. Boston: Kingfisher.

Allington, Richard. 2002. "You Can't Learn Much from Books You Can't Read." *Education Leadership*: 16–19.

Allington, Richard. 2002. "What I've Learned About Effective Reading Instruction from a Decade of Studying Exemplary Elementary Classroom Teachers." *Phi Delta Kappan*, no. 83 (June): 740–47.

Allington, Richard L. 2005. *What Really Matters for Struggling Readers: Designing Research-Based Programs*. 2nd ed. New York: Longman.

Anderson, Carl. 2005. *Assessing Writers*. Portsmouth, NH: Heinemann.

APA Style. 2012. *APA Style*. Retrieved November 20, 2011, from http://www.apastyle.org.

Baumann, James F., and Ann M. Duffy. 1997. *Engaged Reading for Pleasure and Learning: A Report from the National Reading Research Center*. Athens, GA: National Reading Research Center.

Bomer, Katherine. 2010. *Hidden Gems: Naming and Teaching from the Brilliance in Every Student's Writing*. Portsmouth, NH: Heinemann.

Bomer, Katherine. 2005. *Writing a Life: Teaching Memoir to Sharpen Insight, Shape Meaning—and Triumph Over Tests*. Portsmouth, NH: Heinemann.

Booth, Wayne C., Gregory G. Colomb, and Joseph M. Williams. 2003. *The Craft of Research: From Planning to Reporting*. Chicago: University of Chicago Press.

Bransford, John. 2000. *How People Learn: Brain, Mind, Experience, and School*. Washington, DC: National Academy Press.

Budiansky, S. 2001. "The Trouble with Textbooks." *Prism* 10, no. 6: 24–27.

Calkins, Lucy. 2006. *A Guide to the Writing Workshop*. Portsmouth, NH: Heinemann.

Calkins, Lucy, et al. 2006. *Units of Study for Teaching Writing, Grades 3–5*. Portsmouth, NH: Heinemann.

Calkins, Lucy. 1994. *The Art of Teaching Writing, New Edition*. Portsmouth, NH: Heinemann.

Calkins, Lucy, and Kathleen Tolan. 2010. *Units of Study for Teaching Reading, Grades 3–5: Navigating Nonfiction*. Portsmouth, NH: Heinemann.

Calkins, Lucy, Mary Ehrenworth, and Christopher Lehman. 2012. *Pathways to the Common Core: Accelerating Achievement*. Portsmouth, NH: Heinemann.

Carnegie Corporation. 2007. *Writing Next*. Report.

Flaherty, Francis. 2009. *The Elements of Story: Field Notes on Nonfiction Writing*. New York: Harper.

Francois, Chantal, and Elisa Zonana. 2009. *Catching Up on Conventions: Grammar Lessons for Middle School Writers*. Portsmouth, NH: Heinemann.

Fried, Ellen. 2004. *Stars and Galaxies*. Washington, DC: National Geographic Society.

Gibaldi, J. 2009. *MLA Handbook for Writers of Research Papers*. 7th ed. New York: Modern Language Association of America. Print.

Gibbons, Pauline. 2009. "Scaffolding Academic Language and Literacy in the Middle Years." Lecture, Teachers College, Columbia University, New York, November 24.

Gilmore, Barry. 2008. *Plagiarism: Why It Happens, How to Prevent It*. Portsmouth, NH: Heinemann. Print.

Gladwell, Malcolm. 2008. "Most Likely to Succeed." *New Yorker*. Web.

Gladwell, Malcolm. 2008. *Outliers: The Story of Success*. New York: Little, Brown and Co.

Goodall, Jane. 2001. *The Chimpanzees I Love: Saving Their World and Ours*. New York: Scholastic Press.

Harvey, Stephanie. 1998. *Nonfiction Matters: Reading, Writing, and Research in Grades 3–8*. York, ME: Stenhouse Publishers. Print.

Harvey, Stephanie, and Anne Goudvis. 2007. *Strategies That Work: Teaching Comprehension for Understanding and Engagement*. Portland, ME: Stenhouse Publishers.

Harvey, Stephanie, and Harvey Daniels. 2009. *Comprehension & Collaboration: Inquiry Circles in Action*. Portsmouth, NH: Heinemann.

Hattie, John. 2008. *Visible Learning: A Synthesis of Over 800 Meta-Analyses Relating to Achievement*. London: Routledge.

Hess, Karin, and SMARTER Balanced. "Draft: Content Specifications with Content Mapping for the Summative Assessment of the Common Core State Standards for English Language Arts & Literacy in History/Social Studies, Science, and Technical Subjects and Appendices A–C." 19 Sept. 2011. http://www.smarterbalanced.org /wordpress/wp-content/uploads/2011/12/ELA-LiteracyContentSpecifications.pdf

Home: Oxford English Dictionary. Accessed December 21, 2011. http://www.oed.com /view/Entry/163432.

Johnson, Rebecca L. 2003. *Looking at Cells*. Washington, DC: National Geographic Society.

Kuhn, Deanna. 2005. *Education for Thinking*. Cambridge, MA: Harvard University Press.

Lehman, Christopher. 2011. *A Quick Guide to Reviving Disengaged Writers, 5–8*. Portsmouth, NH: Heinemann. Print.

Levitt, Steven D., and Stephen J. Dubner. 2005. *Freakonomics: A Rogue Economist Explores the Hidden Side of Everything*. New York: William Morrow.

Marrin, Albert, and C. B. Mordan. 2006. *Oh, Rats!: The Story of Rats and People*. New York: Dutton Children's Books.

McMillan, Beverly, and John A. Musick. 2008. *Sharks*. New York: Simon & Schuster Books for Young Readers.

Murray, Don. 1978. "Write Before Writing." *College Composition and Communication* 29, no. 4 (December): 375–81.

National Governors Association Center for Best Practices and the Council of Chief State School Officers. "Common Core State Standards Initiative | The Standards | English Language Arts Standards." *Common Core State Standards Initiative | Home*. Web. 12 Aug. 2011. http://www.corestandards.org/the-standards/english-language-arts-standards.

Pantell, Robert H., James F. Fries, and Donald M. Vickery. 1977. *Taking Care of Your Child: A Parent's Guide to Medical Care*. Reading, MA: Addison-Wesley.

Partnership for Assessment of Readiness for College and Careers. "Frequently Asked Questions: PARCC Item Development Procurement & Assessment Development." Web. 15 Dec. 2011. www.parcconline.org/sites/parcc/files/PARCC Item Development ITN FAQs - Updated 01-09-12.pdf.

Peynaud, Emile, and Jacques Blouin. 1996. *The Taste of Wine: The Art and Science of Wine Appreciation*. New York: Wiley.

Pollan, Michael. 2006. *The Omnivore's Dilemma: A Natural History of Four Meals*. New York: Penguin Press.

Portalupi, JoAnn, and Ralph J. Fletcher. 2001. *Nonfiction Craft Lessons: Teaching Information Writing K–8*. Portland, ME: Stenhouse Publishers.

Pransky, Ken. 2010. "How Can We Develop a Conceptually-Based, Enormously Practical Approach to Vocabulary?" Lecture, Teachers College, Columbia University, New York, October 20.

Ray, Katie Wood. 1999. *Wondrous Words: Writers and Writing in the Elementary Classroom.* Urbana, IL: National Council of Teachers of English.

Schmidt, Laurel J. 2007. *Social Studies That Sticks: How to Bring Content and Concepts to Life.* Portsmouth, NH: Heinemann.

"Science Bytes: Whisker Wonders." 2011. *PBS Video.* Web. 15 Dec. http://video.pbs.org /video/2070435179/.

Turabian, Kate L. 2007. *A Manual for Writers of Research Papers, Theses, and Dissertations: Chicago Style for Students and Researchers.* 7th ed. Chicago: University of Chicago Press. Print.

Welcome to the Purdue University Online Writing Lab (OWL). Web. 20 Nov. 2011. http://owl.english.purdue.edu/.